THE ULTIMATE GUIDE TO
DOGS

THE ULTIMATE GUIDE TO
DOGS

David Alderton

Bath · New York · Singapore · Hong Kong · Cologne · Delhi · Melbourne

First published by Parragon in 2009

Parragon

Queen Street House

4 Queen Street

Bath BA1 1HE, UK

Created and produced by

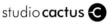
studio cactus

13 SOUTHGATE STREET   WINCHESTER   HAMPSHIRE   SO23 9DZ

DESIGN Laura Watson, Sharon Rudd

EDITORIAL Jennifer Close

ISBN: 978-1-4075-5529-4

Printed in China

STUDIO CACTUS WOULD LIKE TO THANK
Sharon Cluett for original styling; Jo Weeks for proofreading; Penelope Kent for indexing; and Candida Frith-MacDonald for additional text

PICTURE CREDITS
All images © Tracy Morgan Animal Photography, except:
Abramova Kseniya 4 l; Aleksander Bochenek 78 b r; Aleksey Ignatenko 76 b l; alexan55 49 t r, 49 b l; Andrew Williams 58 b; Animal Photography 53 b, 61 b r; Annette 35 t l; Artur Zinatullin 49 b r; Corbis Images 52 t, 61 t l; cynoclub 37 b r, 82 t r; Studio Cactus 33 b l, 33 b r, 38 t l, 38 b r, 39 l, 41 b, 47 t l, 47 r, 47 b l, 52 b l, 52 b r, 53 t, 59 b, 60 t, 60 b, 62 t r, 62 b l, 64 t, 64 b, 65 t, 65 b r, 67 b, 68 t l, 68 b l, 69 t r, 70 b l, 70 b r, 71 c r, 72 b, 78 t l, 78 t l, 81 b l, 85 t, 87 b l, 90 t r, 92 b l, 92 b r, 94 b l; Diane Critelli 10 t r; DK Images 84 b l; Eline Spek 14; Eric Isselée 23 b, 33 t, 37 b l, 45 b , 46 t r, 73 t r, 80 t, 80 b l, 81 t r, 83 b r, 85 b, 92 t r; Erik Lam 21 t l, 66 t r, 87 t l, 87 t r; Gemmav D. Stokes 40 b; Getty Images 32 b, 35 b l, 42 t r, 46 b l, 56 b, 71 b l, 79 t; Hedser van Brug 11 t r, 54 b; ingret 21 b l; Ingvald Kaldhussater 86 b; iofoto 28 t r; iofoto 35 t r, 39 b r; istock 44 b; Iztok Noc 73 b r; Jacqueline Abromeit 42 t l; James Klotz 54 t l; Jay Crihfield 34 b l; Jeffrey Ong Guo Xiong 77 b l; Joy Brown 23 t r; Kirk Geisler 12 b l, 66 b l; Kristian Sekulic 2–3; Laurie Lindstrom 48; Marc Henrie, ASC 82 b, 89 t, 89 b; Mary E. Cioffi 9 t r; Matthew Collingwood 78 b l; Michael Ledray 17 t; Michal Napartowicz 43 t r; N Joy Neish 13 c r; NHPA 6, 12 b, 24; Nicholas James Homrich 94 b r; Nicholas Peter Gavin Davies 25 t; Pavel Bortel 20 t r, 20 b; Pedro Jorge Henriques Monteiro 8 b; photos.com 62 b r, 88 b r, 90 b, 91 c l, 94 t; pixshots 65 b l; Rebecca Schulz 91 t r; Rhonda ODonnell 29 t r, 91 b; Rolf Klebsattel 74 t r; Sergey I 9 b l; Shutterstock.com 13 t, 95 t r; Sklep Spozywczy 21 b r; Sonja Foos 31 t r; Steven Pepple 42 b; stoupa 66 b r; Susan Harris 9 b l; Tad Denson 11 b r, 87 b r; vnlit 32 t l, 32 t r; Waldemar Dabrowski 26 b l, 35 b r, 57 b, 74 b l; Werner Stoffberg 10 b l; WizData, inc. 28 b; wojciechpusz 43 b; zimmytws 69 b.

COVER IMAGES: Main Image: Yellow Labrador Retriever © Mark Raycroft/Minden Pictures/Gettyimages. Right hand side/back image: Grassland © Corbis. Bottom left to right: West Highland White Terrier © Steven Pepple; Basset Hound © Sean MacLeay; British Bulldog © Claudia Steininger

CONTENTS

ABOUT THIS BOOK

There is no universal system of breed classification for dogs but, generally, they are divided on the basis of their original function. Some categories such as the hound group are more natural than others, which may simply consist of breeds with diverse working ancestries. Not all breeds are recognized for show purposes, and recognition can vary between different organizations and countries.

BREED RECOGNITION

The divisions used in this book are linked to those employed by kennel clubs around the world, with acceptance by the U.K.'s Kennel Club (KC), the Fédération Cynologique Internationale (FCI), and the various American Kennel Clubs (AKCs) being listed under the individual entries.

This is not to say that judging standards are the same in each case, however, because these do vary between organizations, and in turn affect the judging process itself. In some instances, although dogs may exist in a wide range of colors, this does not mean that all varieties are universally accepted for show purposes.

COAT COLORS

The coat color swatches that accompany the individual entries give a guide to the colors and color combinations linked with particular breeds, but should not be interpreted literally in all cases. The cream swatch, as an example, describes breeds with very pale coats, whose coloration may range from white through to a dark shade of cream. More precise individual information about the colors associated with a particular breed can be found in the fact box accompanying the entry, although bear in mind that not all colors or coat variants are equally common within a breed. On the other hand, in some cases, as with the Golden Retriever, coat coloration can actually be a defining feature of the breed.

SYMBOLS IN THE BOOK

Aside from providing information about the size to which a dog of a particular breed will grow, its coat type, and its level of activity, these symbols can also assist in choosing a breed that will match your requirements. The height of most breeds is standard, but bear in mind that in the case of bigger breeds, bitches usually grow to a slightly smaller size than male dogs. Also, the level of exercise that an individual dog requires will be affected both by its age and its overall state of health.

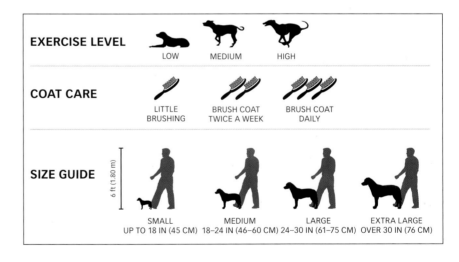

EXERCISE LEVEL	LOW	MEDIUM	HIGH

COAT CARE	LITTLE BRUSHING	BRUSH COAT TWICE A WEEK	BRUSH COAT DAILY

SIZE GUIDE	SMALL UP TO 18 IN (45 CM)	MEDIUM 18–24 IN (46–60 CM)	LARGE 24–30 IN (61–75 CM)	EXTRA LARGE OVER 30 IN (76 CM)

6 ft (1.80 m)

COAT COLORS

BLACK	CREAM	GRAY	BLUE	RED/TAN	GOLD	DARK BROWN

GOLD AND WHITE	BLACK AND WHITE	TAN AND WHITE	BLACK AND TAN	BLACK, WHITE, AND TAN	BLUE MOTTLED WITH TAN	BLACK BRINDLE

THE ORIGINS OF BREEDS

What sets the dog apart from all other domestic animals is the way it has adapted, in terms of its association with us. Dogs have performed a very wide range of roles through history, mirroring the changes that have taken place in human society down through the millennia, and have been bred to fit these different niches. This is an ongoing process, as reflected by the growing number of so-called "designer dogs" now being created.

HUNTERS AND GUARDIANS

At the outset, dogs were kept as hunting companions, helping to provide food, in addition to acting as guardians around settlements. Then, once agriculture started to develop, dogs were used to herd and guard livestock. Their role as hunting companions continued to diversify, and when shooting became a fashionable pastime in the 1800s, breeds of dog were created specially as gundogs. It is the adaptability of the dog that has seen their skills being used in a wide range of different activities.

The most significant change to date started in the late 1800s. The increasing mechanization that was taking place in Europe and North America gave many people more leisure time and greater wealth, as reflected by a growing middle class. This was a time of evolutionary theory, and people were embarking on selective breeding of a wide range of plants and animals, which became known as "fancying." The results of such endeavors were seen at shows.

THE SHOW SCENE

Up until this stage, there had been no breeds as such but, rather, dogs had developed recognizable characteristics linked to their work. The breed concept of today arose in conjunction with the show scene.

Dogs are categorized at shows according to a clear format. The breeds are divided up into different breed groups, such as hounds, that reflect their origins. Then within each breed division, there will be various "classes" depending on the size of the show and its popularity. Class winners compete for the best of breed title, and each of these then progress to best in group. Finally, these winners compete for the best in show award, each being judged against their individual breed standard.

SPANIEL Extremely versatile and generally very friendly, working spaniels track down prey and flush it out for the waiting hunters. They then use scent to find the fallen quarry and retrieve it.

SETTING THE STANDARD

The ideal example of each breed is encapsulated in the breed standard, which is laid down by the registration body, such as the Kennel Club (KC) in the United Kingdom, or the Fédération Cynologique Internationale (FCI) in mainland Europe. The situation is more confused in the United States since there are a number of separate registration bodies, of which the best known is the American Kennel Club. The standard is an attempt to portray in words a description of what the breed should look like, in all respects, including coloration.

DESIGNER DOGS

A popular growing trend in dog breeding is what are now being called "designer dogs," the result of crosses between existing purebreds with the aim of capturing the most desirable traits of both parents. Designer dogs may represent a new breed category for show purposes in the future. Although this type of breeding has a novelty value, it is simply a continuation of the same trend that has taken place since the very start of the domestication of the dog.

Breeders creating true designer dogs are usually aiming to refine the personalities and characteristics of these dogs so as to make them better companions, which is the main role of the dog today. Quiet, cute, small, and trainable are just some of the characteristics that are usually favored. The range of designer dogs continues to increase, with over 75 such crosses having been named to date. The trend is now firmly established to combine parts of the name of both ancestral breeds in that of the designer dog. Hence Labradoodle, reflecting a cross

PUGGLE The increasingly popular Puggle is a designer crossbreed created by crossing the Pug and the Beagle. The result is a good-natured, active, and playful companion breed with a distinctive and endearing expression.

between a Labrador Retriever and a Poodle, a Cock-a-poo, which is the result of a Cocker Spaniel–Poodle ancestry, or a Puggle, a cross between a Pug and a Beagle.

Poodles have played the most significant role so far in the ancestry of designer dogs, partly because they do not shed their fur, so seem to be less likely to trigger an allergic reaction in people who are sensitive. This hypoallergenic aspect can be critical especially for disabled people, who may otherwise be deprived of canine assistance. In fact, Labradoodles—currently the best known of the designer dogs—were originally created for this reason to aid those with impaired sight.

SHOWING THE SAME BREED Depending on the size of the show, there will be various classes within each actual breed division, such as classes for puppies, or for older, "veteran" dogs.

LABRADOODLE The general aim with crosses of this type is to create a dog with a fairly individual appearance, while selecting for desirable traits and behavior.

COMPANION DOGS, TERRIERS, AND HOUNDS

These three groups of dogs cover a wide diversity from tiny companions to independent terriers and gregarious hounds, and range from the oldest sighthound breeds in the world to newly created and refined canine companions. What they all share is popularity with pet owners, and a relatively easy adaptation to modern lifestyles and new roles.

COMPANION DOGS

Today, many breeds created for a working purpose are kept simply as companions, but for thousands of years humans have bred dogs purely for that role. In a number of cases, companion dogs were effectively smaller examples of larger breeds, often referred to as toy breeds, but miniaturization can lead to a decline in the breed's soundness. They have been bred for submissive docility and affection, while aggression, hunting instincts, and other "awkward" traits have been quietly sidelined.

MODERN COMPANIONS

Having been bred over the course of centuries to act as companions, the toy breeds are ideally suited to domestic

BICHON It is possible to track the Bichon lineage back thousands of years, with these small companion dogs all being distinguished by their white, fluffy coats. They are today's most popular companion breed.

living. They are generally very intelligent and responsive by nature, making them easier to train than larger dogs created for working purposes. Their exercise needs are modest and so they are ideally suited to modern-day urban life. They are a good choice for older owners, because their size means they are easy to pick up when necessary. Their lifespan is also likely to be longer than that of larger breeds.

TERRIERS

Dogs have always had a natural tendency to hunt, and this instinct remains strong in the case of the terrier breeds. They were created as industrious, hardy farm dogs, and still display great stamina. These little dogs were miniaturized from hounds to follow prey underground—their name comes from *terre*, French for "earth"—and kill it or drag it out. This work required dogs small in size but big in spirit. Some are still kept on farms for their working abilities.

Most terriers are versatile hunters, capable of ambushing unwary rabbits, although being employed more commonly to hunt down and kill rodents around the farm. In the 19th century, public ratting contests showcased this ability. Other even more macabre forms of entertainment were developed in the growing industrial cities. Dog fighting became popular, with the tenacity and bravery

ACTIVE It is important not to be fooled by their size, because terriers generally need plenty of exercise, possessing great stamina. They can also prove to be rather obstinate by nature, and need sound training.

of terriers putting them in the front line of such contests. Breeds that were developed for this purpose include the Staffordshire Bull Terrier.

MODERN TERRIERS

As there has been less need for working terriers over recent years, their numbers have fallen to the extent that some breeds now face an uncertain future. Others, notably those that have been miniaturized even further, such as the Yorkshire Terrier, often tend to be considered more as companion dogs today.

Terriers are very hardy, long-lived dogs, which thrive in a rural environment. They are generally small in size, and their lively personalities mean they make good companions, especially for older owners. They will also prove alert guardians around the home. However, their rather impatient and often dominant natures mean they are probably not the ideal choice for a home alongside young children, and need sound training to reduce their innate pugnaciousness toward other dogs.

HOUNDS

Hounds represent the oldest group of dogs, having been developed primarily for hunting purposes. They are broadly divided today into sighthounds and scenthounds, reflecting the way in which they pursue their quarry. Most countries have their own breeds of hound, although some of these still remain very localized in their distribution.

Lightly built sighthounds were among the early types to develop, principally in North Africa and the Middle East. Sighthounds have a narrow nose, with their eyes being well positioned toward the sides of the head to help them to identify movement in their vicinity. Most sighthounds tend to hunt individually, or in couples, pursuing their quarry through open countryside where they can maintain visual contact.

The ability to track quarry by scent is required in wooded areas of northern Europe. The development of scenthounds reached its greatest diversity in France, prior to the French Revolution of 1789, when most of the country's châteaux had their own packs of these hounds. A further change occurred with the emergence of the basset forms of many of these breeds. This name originates from the French word *bas*, meaning "low," reflecting the stature of such dogs with their characteristic short-legged appearance.

MODERN HOUNDS

Hounds are lively, friendly, and responsive dogs by nature, ideal for

RACERS Greyhounds are popular today as racing dogs, but they are an ancient type and images of dogs bearing an unmistakable similarity to Greyhounds have been discovered among the artefacts of ancient Egypt.

a home with children. The social nature of most hounds means that they tend to agree well together if you want to keep more than one dog at home. Not all hounds require long walks—Greyhounds, for example, need little more than an opportunity to run in an open field or park for a relatively short time. However, training hounds not to run off when out walking is often difficult, particularly in the case of scenthounds, as they will be instinctively inclined to set off on a trail.

HOUNDS Pack hounds tend to be bicolored or tricolored, usually in a combination of black, white, and tan.

TYPES

Breeds of herding dog have been developed in most parts of the world, and their appearance is influenced to a large extent by the terrain in which they have evolved, usually over the course of centuries. In many instances, they have a dense and often quite long water-resistant coat, which serves to protect them from the worst of the weather.

The dogs in this group are quite variable in size, reflecting their functions. Cattle dogs tend to be small in size, as typified by the Welsh Corgis. This is because they had to be nimble, darting in amongst herds of cattle to nip at the backs of their feet.

In areas where wolves menaced livestock, herd guardians were developed. Not all areas of the world could support a number of different breeds to work with farmstock. This resulted in the development of dogs that could not only herd but also undertake other tasks around the farm.

WORKING DOGS

The description of working dogs is really a catch-all, because with the exception of the companion dogs, all of today's breeds were originally created to undertake specific tasks. Working dogs are friendly and affectionate by nature toward their family circle, and usually prove amenable to training. The large size and strength of many working breeds means that controlling them on a lead may be difficult. They also have large appetites, making them relatively costly to keep. Their maximum lifespan is likely to be shorter than that of smaller breeds, rarely exceeding ten years.

SLED DOGS Siberian Huskies have been replaced in arctic races by the faster Alaskan Husky, but are excellent dogs for moderate loads over long distances.

MASTIFF Recognizable by their large size, stocky bodies, and a wide head with powerful jaws, mastiffs have an overhang of skin around the lips, known as jowls, while the skin on the forehead is wrinkled.

TYPES

This group name covers guarding and rescue breeds, and includes sled-pulling dogs, which had a vital role in moving supplies and people between the remote isolated communities before mechanized transportation. Many members of this group owe their origins to mastiff-type stock—formidable animals with huge heads and powerful jaws that are the ultimate guard dogs. The ancient mastiff bloodline is thought to have begun in the vicinity of China thousands of years ago, and reached Europe along the Old Silk Road. These early mastiffs soon spread widely through Europe, often being used in battle. The overall impression of mastiff breeds is one of tremendous strength.

BREED CATALOGUE

Dogs today are being kept increasingly as companions, rather than for their working abilities. Over the course of little more than a century, their role has altered dramatically, with this change being triggered initially by a growing interest in competitive showing. The original working abilities of breeds have not been neglected though, and there are still field trials where dogs are assessed on these traits rather than on their appearance, which is the case in the show ring. Some dogs compete with equal success in both areas but, increasingly, there has been a divergence in appearance or "type" between working and show dogs of the same breed.

SHETLAND SHEEPDOG Some herding and gundog breeds have separated into down-to-earth working lines and show dogs with features like fuller coats. But many a show Sheltie still combines brains and beauty, scoring well in trials.

Australian Shepherd (Miniature)

ORIGIN United States
HEIGHT 13–18 in (33–45 cm)
WEIGHT 15–30 lb (6.8–13.6 kg)
EXERCISE LEVEL
COAT CARE
REGISTERED None
COLORS Blue or red merle, black, red, may have white and tan markings

Among variations on this breed's name, are the North American Miniature Australian Shepherd, once the North American Shepherd, reflecting the fact that its name and its nationality are at odds.

BLACK   RED/TAN   BLUE MOTTLED WITH TAN

BREED ORIGINS

This breed is descended from the Australian Shepherd, a breed created entirely in the United States using dogs from Australia and New Zealand. That breed was noted for its friendly personality, and so creating a smaller breed that would fit in better with urban lifestyles was a natural step. The smallest of the big breed were selected as breeding stock, and the aim is to produce a perfect miniature in all physical respects, with the same lively and engaging character as the parent. Intelligent and trainable, this is a wonderful dog for an active family, and will relish being allowed to show off in trials.

CITY SLICKER This breed's size means it can be kept comfortably in urban confines, its trainability means it can be well behaved, and it has a low inclination to bark.

Australian Silky Terrier

ORIGIN Australia
HEIGHT 10–11 in (25–28 cm)
WEIGHT 12–14 lb (5.5–6.3 kg)
EXERCISE LEVEL
COAT CARE
REGISTERED KC, FCI, AKCs
COLORS Blue and tan

As much terrier as toy, this breed is similar in appearance to the Yorkshire Terrier, but not quite so diminutive. Although created as a companion breed, it is more than capable of despatching small vermin, and quite feisty when it comes to declaring and defending its interests.

BREED ORIGINS

Although the Australian Silky Terrier only appeared at the turn of the 20th century, its origins are not clearly known. It is probably a cross of the Australian Terrier and the Yorkshire Terrier, possibly with some Skye Terrier thrown in. It can be territorial and independent, so early socialization and obedience training are essential. Given these, this lively and inquisitive breed makes a cheering companion.

STRICTLY DECORATIVE The long coat is fine and silky, and matts easily, so does require daily grooming. Despite its length, it is not insulating, because it lacks an undercoat, so this is a warm-weather breed.

Bichon Frisé

ORIGIN Tenerife
HEIGHT 9–12 in (23–30 cm)
WEIGHT 10–16 lb (4.5–7.2 kg)
EXERCISE LEVEL
COAT CARE
REGISTERED KC, FCI, AKCs
COLORS White

These playful dogs have been popular companions for centuries, and make excellent family pets. The breed's fluffy appearance stems from its distinctive double-layered silky coat.

BREED ORIGINS
It is thought that the Bichon Frisé is descended from the ancient European water spaniel called the Barbet. This is reflected by its name, which is an abbreviated form of Barbichon, translating as "Little Barbet." The breed is also called the Tenerife Dog, and the Bichon Tenerife, reflecting the fact that its development took place on this island, part of the Canaries group off the northwest coast of

Africa. Its ancestors were probably introduced there from Spain over 500 years ago. They became highly sought-after pets at the royal courts of Europe, before gradually falling out of favor and ending up as circus performers. The breed's name is pronounced "Beeshon Freezay."

SNOW WHITE The coat of this breed is naturally curly. It is trimmed back on the face, and this serves to emphasize the round, dark eyes.

Bolognese

ORIGIN Italy
HEIGHT 10–12 in (25–30 cm)
WEIGHT 6–9 lb (2.7–4.1 kg)
EXERCISE LEVEL
COAT CARE
REGISTERED FCI
COLORS White

Although closely related to the Bichon Frisé, the Bolognese differs significantly because its coat is not double layered, although it does stick up rather than lie flat. This is described as "flocking," and gives the breed its fluffy appearance.

BREED ORIGINS
The precise ancestry of the Bolognese is something of a mystery. Its closest relative within the Bichon group is the Maltese, but it is unclear whether the Maltese is its direct ancestor or descendant. The Bolognese's origins date back to around A.D. 1000, with the breed then evolving in the Italian city of Bologna, from which its name is derived. The Medici family in Italy

gave these dogs as gifts to obtain favors and many European rulers fell under their charm.

Part of the Bolognese's undoubted appeal, aside from its attractive appearance, is the very strong bond that these dogs form with their owners.

ONLY WHITE While today, only white examples of the Bolognese are known, both black and piebald examples were recorded at an earlier stage in its history.

Cavalier King Charles Spaniel

ORIGIN United Kingdom

HEIGHT 12 in (30 cm)

WEIGHT 12–18 lb (5.5–8.1 kg)

EXERCISE LEVEL

COAT CARE

REGISTERED KC, FCI, AKCs

COLORS Black and tan, Blenheim, ruby, tricolor

This breed has an attractive appearance and pleasant disposition. They are not particularly energetic dogs, so they are suited to city life, and ideal for a home with children.

RED/TAN   TAN AND WHITE   BLACK AND TAN   BLACK, WHITE, AND TAN

BREED ORIGINS

Small spaniel-type dogs became very fashionable in Britain during the late 1600s, being favorites of King Charles II, as is clear from contemporary paintings. Subsequently, however, their appearance began to change. The modern breed owes its existence to a rich American called Roswell Eldridge. During the 1920s, he put up substantial prize money at Crufts for examples of the King Charles Spaniel or English Toy Spaniel, which resembled the original 17th-century type. Over the five years of Roswell's involvement with the show, the number of such dogs being exhibited increased, and gradually, this type of spaniel became more popular. It was then recognized as the Cavalier King Charles Spaniel, to separate it from its now relatively scarce close relative. The most evident distinguishing feature between the breeds is the longer nose displayed by the Cavalier.

TRICOLOR Black and white is predominant in this coloring, with these colors being evenly distributed. Tan markings show above the eyes, on the cheeks, and in the ears.

BLENHEIM This coloring is the most popular variety, having been originally created on and named after the Duke of Marlborough's estate. Rich chestnut coloring is separated by individual white markings, with a white central area usually evident on the center of the head.

BLACK AND TAN These puppies display their raven-black coloring, offset with tan markings. The other variety is ruby—a rich red shade.

Chihuahua

ORIGIN Mexico
HEIGHT 6–9 in (15–23 cm)
WEIGHT 2–6 lb (1.0–2.7 kg)
EXERCISE LEVEL
COAT CARE (sh) (lh)
REGISTERED KC, FCI, AKCs
COLORS No restrictions on color or patterning

The smallest breed in the world, the distinctive-looking Chihuahua possesses the character and bark of a much larger dog. They are noisy by nature, and have a fearless temperament.

BLACK   CREAM   GRAY   BLUE   RED/TAN

BREED ORIGINS

The Chihuahua is named after the province in Mexico where it originated, but its ancestry remains mysterious. It may be a descendant of a range of companion breeds which were kept throughout the Americas in the pre-Colombian era. Others suggest that its ancestors might have been brought from Spain by the early settlers, and may have

SMOOTH-COATED This is the traditional form of the breed, which is characterized by a domed, apple-shaped head. Its large ears are positioned at an angle of about 45 degrees to the head.

interbred with local dogs to create the breed of today. Chihuahuas first started to attract attention outside Mexico during the 1850s, when they became fashionable companions for wealthy U.S. women, and even today, the breed enjoys celebrity status.

LONGCOATED The coat is soft, with the hair forming a very evident plume on the tail. Longer fur is evident too on the sides of the face, and on the underparts of the body, with feathering on the legs. The coat itself lies flat.

Coton de Tuléar

ORIGIN Madagascar
HEIGHT 10–12 in (25–30 cm)
WEIGHT 12–15 lb (5.5–6.8 kg)
EXERCISE LEVEL
COAT CARE
REGISTERED FCI
COLORS White

This breed is one of relatively few to have originated from Africa, and has grown rapidly in popularity over recent years, both in North America and Europe. It is another member of the Bichon group, as reflected partly by its white coat.

BREED ORIGINS

Almost certainly, the ancestors of this breed were brought from Europe to the Madagascan port of Tuléar, as commemorated by its name. This probably occurred as early as the 1600s, and these small dogs soon became status symbols for wealthy people living on this island, which lies off the east coast of Africa. Being bred here in isolation over the course of hundreds of generations, these dogs gradually diverged somewhat in appearance from their ancestors. It was prohibited for all but the nobility to own them, and they remained unknown elsewhere, right up until the 1950s. A small number were then permitted to leave the island and taken to Europe, while in the United States, they were not seen until the mid-1970s.

WET DOG! Although traditionally the coat falls forward over the face, the wet coat reveals the unmistakable Bichon profile. A similar but now extinct breed existed on the island of Réunion.

COAT The rather fluffy, cottony texture of the Coton de Tuléar's coat is a distinctive feature of these dogs. Although white is the traditional color for the breed, individuals with cream or black patches occasionally occur.

French Bulldog

ORIGIN France
HEIGHT 11–12 in (28–30 cm)
WEIGHT 20–28 lb (9.1–12.7 kg)
EXERCISE LEVEL
COAT CARE
REGISTERED KC, FCI, AKCs
COLORS Cream, gold, liver, black and white, black brindle

The bat-like ears and stocky build of the French Bulldog are very distinctive. Its short coat means that grooming is minimal, but it can be prone to snoring, because of its compact facial shape.

CREAM

GOLD

GOLD AND WHITE

BLACK AND WHITE

BLACK BRINDLE

BREED ORIGINS

There used to be a Toy Bulldog breed which was widely kept by lacemakers in the English city of Nottingham. Forced out by increased mechanization, during the 1850s many of these skilled craftspeople emigrated to northern France. Not surprisingly, they took their pets with them, and some crossbreeding with local dogs occurred. Crosses with terriers may have resulted in the raised ears that are so characteristic

BLACK AND WHITE The markings may be very variable, as can be seen by comparing this example with the dog on the right.

of the breed today. Word of these bulldogs spread to the city of Paris, and soon they became fashionable pets in the capital. They became popular too in other parts of Europe and especially the United States, but in Britain, the breed proved controversial when it was first introduced during the 1890s.

GOOD COMPANION
The French Bulldog is a lively, friendly breed with relatively modest exercise needs.

BRINDLE Mixing of light and dark hairs in the coat is not uncommon in French Bulldogs, as is a white patch on the chest.

German Spitz

ORIGIN Germany
HEIGHT 8–16 in (20–41 cm)
WEIGHT 7–40 lb (3.2–18.0 kg)
EXERCISE LEVEL
COAT CARE
REGISTERED KC, FCI, AKCs
COLORS Range of solid colors; bicolors allowed in Miniature and Toy

The family of German Spitz breeds can be separated by size, with the Giant being the largest. There is also a Standard variety, as well as Miniature and Toy forms. They are all similar in temperament.

BLACK   CREAM   GRAY   GOLD   DARK BROWN

BREED ORIGINS

The origins of the German Spitz date back at least to 1450, and since then, as in the case of other breeds, there has been a tendency to scale these dogs down in size, creating companion breeds. There is also frequently confusion between the German Toy Spitz and the Pomeranian, because they share a common ancestry and are very similar in appearance. The German breed was created first, with the Pomeranian subsequently being

FULL COAT The ruff of fur around the neck is more pronounced in the winter, when the coat is at its most profuse. This contrasts with the short hair on the lower part of the legs.

developed on separate lines in the United Kingdom, from imported German stock, to the extent that they have now existed as separate bloodlines for over a century. There are some differences in the recognition of the different Spitz breeds as far as coloration is concerned. The Giant variety exists in solid colors only, while bicolors are also seen in the case of the Miniature and Toy variants.

FACIAL APPEARANCE The German Spitz breeds are described as being vulpine, or fox-like, as a result of their facial appearance. A white blaze between the eyes is often a feature of bicolors.

Havanese

ORIGIN Cuba

HEIGHT 8–14 in (20–36 cm)

WEIGHT 7–13 lb (3.2–5.9 kg)

EXERCISE LEVEL

COAT CARE

REGISTERED FCI

COLORS Black, white, blue, gold, dark brown

Lively by nature but easy to train, the Havanese has established a following that extends far beyond Cuba where it developed. They are versatile companions, watchdogs, and even poultry herders.

BLACK   CREAM   BLUE   GOLD   DARK BROWN

BREED ORIGINS

The Havanese is of Bichon stock, with its ancestors probably having been introduced to Cuba quite early during the settlement of the New World, when the island was a significant stopping-off point for ships from Europe. The breed is named after Havana, Cuba's capital city. They thrived on the island for centuries, but became much rarer after the Communist takeover in 1959. Many of those who fled to the United States took their Havanese with them, and this actually boosted the breed's popularity in North America. Today, they are seen at shows around the world.

COAT The Havanese's coat has a soft texture and, as with other Bichons, tends to be white in color. The muzzle of these dogs is long and tapered.

STYLING The longer hair on the head reflects the breed's origins in a hot climate, protecting the eyes from the sun. It is traditionally tied up into a topknot.

King Charles Spaniel

ORIGIN United Kingdom
HEIGHT 10–11 in (25–28 cm)
WEIGHT 8–14 lb (3.5–6.3 kg)
EXERCISE LEVEL
COAT CARE
REGISTERED KC, FCI, AKCs
COLORS Solid tan, black and tan, white and tan, tricolor

Despite its spaniel name, this has never been a gundog, but was a royal toy. Diarist Samuel Pepys noted of King Charles "the silliness of the King, playing with his dog all the while."

RED/TAN

BLACK, WHITE, AND TAN

BREED ORIGINS

When spaniels were first developed, larger pups were chosen for working dogs, but smaller ones eventually became toy companion breeds. Early examples had a longer muzzle, like the Cavalier King Charles today, but crossing with snub-nosed oriental breeds in the 18th century gave it a new look.

An affectionate dog that fits well into urban life, the King Charles

Spaniel's drawback is that it is prone to health problems and shorter lived than many small dogs.

ROYAL COLORS This breed's colors have regal names. Tan is called ruby and tan and white Blenheim, and in the United States tricolor is Prince Charles and black and tan is King Charles.

Lhasa Apso

ORIGIN Tibet
HEIGHT 10–11 in (25–28 cm)
WEIGHT 13–15 lb (5.9–6.8 kg)
EXERCISE LEVEL
COAT CARE
REGISTERED KC, FCI, AKCs
COLORS Range of colors from black to cream; black and white

The long, flowing coat of the Lhasa Apso is very elegant, but its condition can only be maintained with daily grooming sessions. Occasionally, a smooth-coated individual crops up in a litter.

BLACK   CREAM   GRAY   GOLD   BLACK AND WHITE

BREED ORIGINS

These small dogs were considered sacred by the Tibetan monks who kept them in their monasteries. They were believed to be a repository for the souls of dead monks. Unsurprisingly, therefore, Lhasa Apsos were not sold to outsiders. Occasionally, however, the Dalai Lama who ruled Tibet would give a pair as a gift to the Chinese Emperor. It was probably

not until the late 19th or early 20th century that the breed first reached the West, and it was not until after World War I that it started to become established in Britain. This proved to be a protracted process, with these striking dogs not becoming well known until the 1960s.

COAT The Lhasa's hair is very dense, and offers excellent protection against the elements.

Löwchen

ORIGIN France
HEIGHT 10–13 in (25–33 cm)
WEIGHT 10–18 lb (4.5–8.1 kg)
EXERCISE LEVEL
COAT CARE
REGISTERED KC, FCI
COLORS No restrictions on color or patterning

When its coat is trimmed, the Löwchen looks rather like a lion, justifying its alternative description of Little Lion Dog. Its name is pronounced as "lerv-chun," and it is a very ancient breed.

BLACK   CREAM   RED/TAN   DARK BROWN   TAN AND WHITE

BREED ORIGINS

It is believed that the breed was widely known across Europe as long ago as the 1500s and, in spite of its Germanic name, the Löwchen's origins are believed to lie in France. The coat was trimmed into the lion-cut, which removes hair from the lower body and upper legs, so that they could act as bed warmers for the nobility, while the resulting leonine appearance was believed to convey strength. In 1973, numbers of the breed had plummeted to the extent that it was estimated that there were fewer than 70 still alive in the world. Thanks to publicity surrounding their plight, breeders have successfully taken up the challenge of preserving this breed.

UNTRIMMED In the Löwchen's untrimmed state, its Bichon family resemblance is clear.

Maltese

ORIGIN Malta
HEIGHT 9–10 in (23–25 cm)
WEIGHT 4–13 lb (1.8–5.9 kg)
EXERCISE LEVEL
COAT CARE
REGISTERED KC, FCI, AKCs
COLORS White

Although it was once called the Maltese Terrier, there has never been anything of the terrier about this breed; it has also been called, more understandably, the Bichon Maltais. It is an engaging little dog, seemingly without fear or awareness of its diminutive size.

BREED ORIGINS

This breed has been kept as a companion since Phoenicians brought the ancient Melita breed to Malta 2000 years ago. A pure line of descent from that dog is unlikely, and today's Maltese probably has both miniature spaniels and the Miniature Poodle in its heritage. It is active and playful, but with maturity adapts to a more sedentary lifestyle and city life. It is good with children or other dogs.

PERFECTLY COIFFED The long silky coat lacks an undercoat and mats easily. The demands of daily grooming are the biggest commitment with this breed.

Papillon

ORIGIN France
HEIGHT 8–11 in (20–28 cm)
WEIGHT 9–10 lb (4.0–4.5 kg)
EXERCISE LEVEL
COAT CARE
REGISTERED KC, FCI, AKCs
COLORS White with a range of colors

It may look like a stuffed toy, have a name meaning butterfly in French, and have been a favorite prop for romantic portraits, but this breed is no brainless lapdog: The fluff is all on the outside.

GOLD AND WHITE

BLACK AND WHITE

TAN AND WHITE

BLACK, WHITE, AND TAN

BREED ORIGINS

These small companions date back to the Renaissance under the name Continental Spaniel, and are still called Continental Toy Spaniels. They may be descended from the Spanish Dwarf Spaniel of the 16th century, crossed with northern spitz types for a more delicate face. While its history is not well recorded in writing, it was a favorite in works of art, depicted in frescoes and oil paintings from Titian's *Venus of Urbino* to Largillière's portrait of Louis XIV and his family. In many of these, the structure of the dogs' ears is unclear, and it seems that

DOGS WITH WINGS
At first, calling a dog "butterfly" might not seem descriptive, but a glance at the ears and facial markings makes it clear how apt the name is.

the Papillon appeared in the 16th century, with the original drop-eared type being given the name of Phalène sometime later in order to distinguish them.

BREED QUALITIES

With their fine, silky coat, plumed tail, and extraordinary ears, it is not hard to see why this breed became popular. The coat, which lacks an undercoat, needs less attention than might be expected to keep it looking picture perfect. Papillons can be possessive of their owners and territory, but given an outlet for their energy make engaging companions.

QUICK LEARNER The Papillon loves outdoor exercise, and given a little training, its playful nature and surprising speed and athleticism make it adept at obedience trials, performing tricks, and in agility classes for small dogs.

Pekingese

ORIGIN China
HEIGHT 6–9 in (15–23 cm)
WEIGHT 7–12 lb (3.0–5.5 kg)
EXERCISE LEVEL
COAT CARE
REGISTERED KC, FCI, AKCs
COLORS Any color

According to legend, this breed is the result of a mating between a lion and a monkey. The tale does an equally good job of explaining its appearance or describing its personality.

BLACK

RED/TAN

GOLD

TAN AND
WHITE

BREED ORIGINS

The origins of the Peke are far too distant to be known: It was recently confirmed as one of the world's most ancient breeds by DNA analysis, showing just how long-standing the desire to keep dogs as companions is. It was kept at the Chinese imperial court in the Forbidden City, and brought back to the United Kingdom in the 1860s, having been taken from the court in the Opium Wars. Today, it is a parent of many crossbreeds with names like "Peke-a-Pom."

BREED QUALITIES

This breed behaves as if it is well aware of its royal past. They can be very obstinate, and it is surprising just how heavy such a small dog becomes when it does not wish to go somewhere. Pekingese tend to be loyal to their owners, wary of strangers, and inclined to bark like little watchdogs.

ROYAL RULES This breed is still true to the standard written by Dowager Empress Tzu Hsi, with hairy paws for silence, a color to match every robe, a ruff for dignity, and bow legs to prevent it wandering.

Pomeranian

ORIGIN Germany

HEIGHT 8–11 in (20–28 cm)

WEIGHT 4–7 lb (1.8–3.2 kg)

EXERCISE LEVEL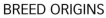

COAT CARE

REGISTERED KC, FCI, AKCs

COLORS White, cream, gray, blue, red, brown, black

It resembles nothing so much as an animated powder puff, but this dog believes it is still as big as its ancestors. The Pomeranian is also called the Zwergspitz or Dwarf Spitz and the Loulou.

BLACK CREAM RED/TAN GOLD

BREED ORIGINS

The Pomeranian takes its name from a region along the Baltic coast that has been part of many countries over the centuries: Once German, it is now in Poland. The German Spitz family was first brought to the United Kingdom by Queen Charlotte at the start of the 19th century, and British breeders succeeded in diminishing its size through the century. This may have been helped by a Volpino

BEST BRUSHED The long, straight coat has a dense undercoat and needs frequent attention with a damp brush to prevent tangles forming.

brought back from Italy by Queen Victoria; her patronage insured the popularity of the fledgling type.

BREED QUALITIES

Smart and energetic, this is a good family companion and suits city life. It is protective of its territory and will bark noisily, so makes an effective watchdog, although unable to do much physical damage to an intruder. It will also challenge larger dogs, seemingly unaware of its size. These are long-lived dogs, although they do suffer from several health problems including slipping kneecaps and eye problems.

COLOR INFLUENCES SIZE The earliest Poms tended to be both white and larger, but as an ever smaller size has been pursued, red and sable tones have become most common.

Poodle (Miniature and Toy)

ORIGIN France
HEIGHT 9–15 in (23–38 cm)
WEIGHT 4–18 lb (1.8–5.5 kg)
EXERCISE LEVEL
COAT CARE
REGISTERED KC, FCI, AKCs
COLORS Any solid color

The full-sized or Standard Poodle can still be seen as a working breed, but these smaller types were created purely for the pleasure of their company.

BLACK   CREAM   BLUE   GOLD   DARK BROWN

BREED ORIGINS
Wherever the full-sized Poodle originated, there is no doubt that the smaller versions of the breed were developed in France. These dogs were never intended to be gundogs, although they will point and show all the instinctive drives of their larger ancestors. They have been, and still are, popular as circus dogs, at least in part for their great intelligence. Since the 18th century they have danced, acted out comedies, tragedies, and battles, reportedly walked tightropes, and even played cards and performed magic tricks, responding to the slightest signals from their trainers.

BREED QUALITIES
If they are allowed, these small poodles will make responsive and entertaining companions. Treated as fashion accessories, they can become bored and destructive. Grooming depends on the clip; some health problems—such as ear infections—can be more troublesome.

KEEPING IT SIMPLE Puppies may be shown in a plain, all-over clip. For adults, show rules are stricter, but there is nothing to stop an owner keeping this easycare look.

TOY POODLE The very smallest of the sizes, this is the ultimate choice for bijou urban homes. The smallest are the longest lived, lasting around 14 years.

MINIATURE POODLE This size was highly popular in the circus ring, and was a must-have pet in the mid-20th century. Overbreeding meant that it slipped from pole position, but this has been a good thing for the quality of the breed.

Pug

ORIGIN China
HEIGHT 10–11 in (25–28 cm)
WEIGHT 14–18 lb (6.4–8.2 kg)
EXERCISE LEVEL
COAT CARE
REGISTERED KC, FCI, AKCs
COLORS Silver, apricot, fawn, black

They look frowning, but these mini mastiffs are full of energy and cheer. The name may come from an old English word for a mischievous devil; some European countries call them "Mops."

BLACK   GRAY   GOLD

BREED ORIGINS

This breed was miniaturized at least 2,000 years ago in China, where it was known as the Lo-Chiang-Sze or Foo, and kept by nobles and monks. In the 16th century it reached Europe on ships of the Dutch East Indies Trading Company, and is said to have saved the life of William of Orange by barking at an assassin. It arrived in the United Kingdom when Dutch royalty took the throne in the 17th century, and remained a royal pet, owned by Queen Victoria.

BREED QUALITIES

The word pugnacious might have been taken from this breed; they are intelligent and can be quite obstinate. Their stare looks defiant and stern, but it masks a playful personality, and a pug can be an enlivening and enchanting companion.

ANCIENT LIKENESS This breed still bears some resemblance to the foo dog or lion dog statues that are seen defensively flanking the doors of palaces and temples in China.

CHANGING FASHIONS The original Pug face, seen in paintings such as Hogarth's self-portrait with his Pug, Trump, was longer. The flat profile of today's dog leads to breathing and eye problems.

CHIC COLORS Pale-colored Pugs were the most fashionable until the 19th century, when traveler and author Lady Brassey is thought to have brought new black dogs back from the East.

Shih Tzu

ORIGIN Tibet/China
HEIGHT 8–11 in (20–28 cm)
WEIGHT 9–16 lb (4.1–7.3 kg)
EXERCISE LEVEL
COAT CARE
REGISTERED KC, FCI, AKCs
COLORS Any color

While the pronunciation of the name is a matter of some dispute and not a little humor, the translation is "lion dog." This breed lives up to it, being courageous and sometimes a little haughty.

BLACK   BLUE   GOLD   BLACK AND WHITE   TAN AND WHITE

BREED ORIGINS

It was thought that this breed was a cross between the Pekingese and the Lhasa Apso, which is what it looks like, but recent DNA analysis showed it to be one of the most ancient breeds in its own right. It seems to have come from Tibet to China, where it became a favorite in the court, and spread from there, which is why it is generally regarded as a Chinese, rather than Tibetan breed. They

FLOWER-LIKE FACE The long hair on the brow, which gives the nickname "Chrysanthemum Dog," can be tied up in a topknot; some owners trim it, but this is not allowed for showing.

PERFECT SYMMETRY Bicolored Shih Tzus are commonly seen, and in this coat a white blaze extending from the nose over the face and head and a white tip to the tail are highly desirable.

arrived in Europe in the early 20th century, and have become well loved and established across the world.

BREED QUALITIES

The abundant coat has a long topcoat and a wooly undercoat, so needs regular and thorough grooming. This is a good-natured family dog, relaxed around other dogs and well-behaved children, although it is occasionally stubborn. It also makes an alert watchdog, and although it is usually quiet indoors, it will bark vociferously at anything it feels is wrong.

BLACK-AND-WHITE ADULT The fine undercoat of the Shih Tzu can become easily matted, so this is definitely not a breed for owners averse to grooming.

Airedale Terrier

ORIGIN United Kingdom
HEIGHT 23 in (58 cm)
WEIGHT 44 lb (20.0 kg)
EXERCISE LEVEL
COAT CARE
REGISTERED KC, FCI, AKCs
COLORS Black and tan

Too large to fit the description of an "earth dog," the Airedale is sometimes called the "King of Terriers." Older names include the Bingley Terrier, pinpointing its earliest roots in Yorkshire, and the Waterside Terrier, because of its otter-hunting past.

BREED ORIGINS
The Airedale is a typical terrier in every respect other than size. A cross of the now-vanished Old English Broken-haired Terrier and the Otterhound, it was bred to pursue prey in the water. It has also been a messenger and police dog, but its notorious stubbornness limits its usefulness.

BEST MATE Airedale owners report them to be loyal, brave, and energetic friends.

STREET FIGHTER Although this breed is quiet indoors and makes a good urban companion, it has a tendency to pick fights with other dogs.

American Pit Bull Terrier

ORIGIN United States
HEIGHT 18–22 in (46–56 cm)
WEIGHT 50–80 lb (22.7–36.4 kg)
EXERCISE LEVEL
COAT CARE
REGISTERED AKCs
COLORS Any color

This is the love-it-or-hate it poster child of the fighting breeds and bull terriers class. It is muzzled, microchipped, and barred from housing complexes, parks, cities, and whole countries.

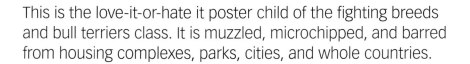

RED/TAN   GOLD AND WHITE   BLACK AND WHITE   TAN AND WHITE   BLACK BRINDLE

BREED ORIGINS
The history of the Pit Bull is that of the American Staffordshire until the mid-20th century, when the two split. The Pit Bull has come off badly: Limited recognition means no strong common breeding policy, while leash laws preclude them from trials in which they used to excel. They are dog-aggressive, but human-aggressive individuals would have been culled in the breed's past, and in the right hands this loyal dog should be less human-aggressive than a mastiff: No powerful dog should be left alone with children.

IMAGE PROBLEM Pit Bulls are too often bought as a macho accessory by owners who encourage aggression, and suffer from the inevitable results. Cropped ears add to the desired "hard" look.

American Staffordshire Terrier

ORIGIN United States
HEIGHT 17–19 in (43–48 cm)
WEIGHT 40–50 lb (18.2–22.7 kg)
EXERCISE LEVEL
COAT CARE
REGISTERED FCI, AKCs
COLORS Any color, with or without white

Not identical to the original Staffordshire Terrier in the United Kingdom, this heftier breed is closer to the American Pit Bull. This fighter is gentle around people, but remorseless with other dogs.

BLACK   DARK BROWN   BLACK AND WHITE   TAN AND WHITE   BLACK AND TAN

BREED ORIGINS
Bull terriers, including the Staffordshire, were brought to the United States in the 19th century and kept as fight and farm dogs. In the 20th century, with fighting outlawed, some turned respectable as Staffies—with "American" added later to avoid confusion with the British breed—while others are known as Pit Bulls. It is still possible for dogs to be registered as one breed in one association and the other elsewhere. Fighting dogs were once renowned for their gentleness around humans, but their owners were experienced handlers who spent much time socializing them as pups; with the same care today, this powerful little dog is an affectionate companion.

SMALL BUT STRONG Although the mastiff guard breeds are bigger, the strong jaws and tenacious grip of these smaller dogs can do as much damage.

Belgian Griffons

ORIGIN Belgium
HEIGHT 7–8 in (18–20 cm)
WEIGHT 7–15 lb (3.2–6.8 kg)
EXERCISE LEVEL
COAT CARE
REGISTERED KC, FCI, AKCs
COLORS Black, red, black and tan

Depending on the registry, these can be one or three breeds. One or all, they are tolerant and amiable companions, gentler than many terriers. Ravaged by two world wars, they remain rare.

BLACK   RED/TAN   BLACK AND TAN

BREED ORIGINS
In Europe, the wirehaired dogs are either Griffon Bruxellois or Griffon Belge according to color, and all the smooth-coated dogs are called Petit Brabançon. Elsewhere, the smooth-coated dogs are a variety within a breed called Brussels Griffon or Griffon Bruxellois. All are descended from the Griffon d'Écurie or Stable Griffon, with probable input from the Affenpinscher, the Dutch Smoushond, the Yorkshire Terrier, toy spaniels from the United Kingdom, and Pugs.

COLOR DISTINCTION (right) The rough, reddish coat makes this a Griffon Bruxellois in Europe; the Griffon Belge is black or black and tan.

LITTLE SMOOTHIES (left) Because "griffon" indicates a rough coat, in Europe these dogs are called Petit Brabançon, after a Belgian province.

Border Terrier

ORIGIN United Kingdom
HEIGHT 10 in (25 cm)
WEIGHT 11–15 lb (5.0–6.8 kg)
EXERCISE LEVEL
COAT CARE
REGISTERED KC, FCI, AKCs
COLORS Gray, wheaten, tan or red, blue and tan

Although it has become a popular family companion, this dog still shows itself to be a true hunting type. It has a compact build, persistent but amenable temperament, and hardy constitution.

GRAY   RED/TAN   GOLD

BREED ORIGINS

Like so many working dogs, this breed comes from undocumented origins. Dogs like these were working in the English-Scottish border area in the late 18th century, killing rats and foxes, and possibly otters and badgers. Their descendants include not only the Border Terrier, but also the less widely recognized Fell and Patterdale Terriers, kept as working dogs. The name Border Terrier was in use for this type by the end of the 19th century, and the breed was recognized in the early 20th century.

BREED QUALITIES

This terrier is popular in the United Kingdom, and is in the top ten breeds. This has happened only recently, and it is less popular elsewhere, so it has not been overbred, and remains true to its original type. It has a more tolerant, less snappy personality than many terriers, and is more trainable and a fine family dog—albeit still terrier enough to need active owners.

PERFECT SIZE The Border is an ideal vermin hunter, leggy enough to run good distances, but small enough to fit down a fox's earth.

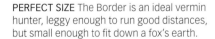

COAT CARE The hard coat is weatherproof and easy to maintain, shedding dirt with a quick brush. A sleeker look is achieved by hand-stripping the dead hair twice a year.

Boston Terrier

ORIGIN United States
HEIGHT 15–17 in (38–43 cm)
WEIGHT 15–25 lb (6.8–11.4 kg)
EXERCISE LEVEL
COAT CARE
REGISTERED KC, FCI, AKCs
COLORS Brindle, seal, or black with white markings

With a heritage of mastiffs and fighting dogs, one might expect this to be a bullish breed, but it is one of the most relaxed breeds to carry the "terrier" label, even something of a layabout.

BLACK AND WHITE   BLACK BRINDLE

BREED ORIGINS

The Boston dates back to the late 19th century and is a blend of old English and French Bulldogs and the now-extinct White Terrier, with constant selection for smaller size. The breed was an immediate success, the first American breed to gain recognition, and has remained a favorite with the public ever since due to its engaging, compliant personality.

TRIM LOOKS The ears are naturally erect and batlike, but are sometimes cropped to "improve" the line. The tail is naturally short, and not now docked.

Bull Terrier

ORIGIN United Kingdom
HEIGHT 21–22 in (53–56 cm)
WEIGHT 52–62 lb (23.6–28.2 kg)
EXERCISE LEVEL
COAT CARE
REGISTERED KC, FCI, AKCs
COLORS Any color except blue or liver

Instantly recognizable for its convex Roman nose, this dog was first developed as a fighting breed. It is usually a trustworthy and stable breed, but no powerful dog is ideal for a novice owner.

BLACK AND WHITE   TAN AND WHITE   BLACK, WHITE, AND TAN   BLACK BRINDLE

BREED ORIGINS

This breed was developed by John Hinks early in the 19th century. He crossed the White English Terrier, now extinct, with the Bulldog, and the result was instantly successful as a fighter and as a companion. Active and highly intelligent, Bull Terriers should be kept busy. They are tolerant, and do not bite readily, but also do not let go easily, and young dogs may play too roughly for children.

ORIGINAL COLOR Hinks preferred white, still the only color allowed in some registries, but it carries an increased risk of deafness and health problems. Head markings are not penalized.

Cairn Terrier

ORIGIN United Kingdom
HEIGHT 9–10 in (23–25 cm)
WEIGHT 13–14 lb (5.9–6.4 kg)
EXERCISE LEVEL
COAT CARE
REGISTERED KC, FCI, AKCs
COLORS Cream, wheaten, red, sandy, gray, brindled

This typically compact, shaggy little terrier from Scotland has long been a popular breed. It has a robust constitution and an equally robust temperament.

CREAM GRAY BLACK BRINDLE

BREED ORIGINS

The exact origins of the Cairn are uncertain, but are almost certainly linked to those of other breeds such as the Scottish, Skye, and West Highland White Terriers. Its name comes from marker cairns built of stones, and its use in hunting out vermin that took refuge in them. Today, it still loves to chase and dig, and may not be for those who love their lawn. It makes a good watchdog and city companion, with a more obedient character than some other terriers. It is cheerful and entertaining, as long as it is entertained in turn.

COAT CARE The hard, wiry top coat of the Cairn can be trimmed around the eyes, but is best "stripped" by hand, or plucked out to reveal the soft undercoat, in summer.

Irish Terrier

ORIGIN Ireland
HEIGHT 18 in (46 cm)
WEIGHT 25–27 lb (11.4–12.3 kg)
EXERCISE LEVEL
COAT CARE
REGISTERED KC, FCI, AKCs
COLORS Yellow, wheaten, red

These are also called Irish Red Terriers or, by their fans, Daredevils. Even the breed standards mention the breed's "heedless, reckless pluck." They are animated hunters and loyal defenders of the home.

RED/TAN GOLD

BREED ORIGINS

These dogs emerged from the general stock of guards and vermin hunters through selective breeding in the 19th century, and by the end of the century they had become the first Irish breed recognized by the Kennel Club and been exported to the United States. Still used for hunting in Ireland, they are more often seen as household and family companions. Provided that they are given enough exercise to use up some of their boundless energy, they can be very civilized indoors: They are tractable with people, but unreliable around dogs or other small pets.

IRISH LOOKS Deeper red coats predominate because they tend to be harder in texture than pale coats. The tail was customarily docked; left natural, it should be held high but not curled over.

Jack Russell Terrier

ORIGIN United Kingdom
HEIGHT 10–12 in (25–30 cm)
WEIGHT 9–15 lb (4–7 kg)
EXERCISE LEVEL
COAT CARE
REGISTERED FCI
COLORS Bicolored or tricolored

These terriers are full of character, and have an adventurous side to their natures that can occasionally lead them into trouble, since they have little fear.

BLACK AND WHITE

BLACK AND TAN

BLACK, WHITE, AND TAN

WELL TRAVELED The first man to walk to both Poles, Ranulph Fiennes, was accompanied by his Jack Russell, Bothie—an extraordinary feat for a British rural hunting breed.

BREED ORIGINS

The Jack Russell Terrier is named after its creator, who obtained a distinctive terrier bitch in May 1819, while studying at Oxford University. He developed a terrier that was bold enough to venture underground to drive out a fox from its earth, and yet could also run well. They were later crossed with a range of other dogs, which helps explain their variable appearance.

BREED QUALITIES

Jack Russell Terriers remain popular, both as companions and working dogs, often being seen on farms. They also prove to be alert watchdogs, with a surprisingly loud bark for their diminutive stature.

PERFECT SIZE To chase foxes into earths, working dogs must never be more than 14 in (35 cm) around the chest.

Kerry Blue Terrier

ORIGIN Ireland
HEIGHT 17–19 in (43–48 cm)
WEIGHT 33–40 lb (15.0–18.2 kg)
EXERCISE LEVEL
COAT CARE
REGISTERED KC, FCI, AKCs
COLORS Blue

Also known as the Irish Blue Terrier, this breed was first noted in Kerry in the southwest, but never restricted to that corner of Ireland. It is traditionally the national dog of Ireland, but surprisingly rare for a breed with such status.

BREED ORIGINS

The origins of this breed are uncertain, and ancestors may include the Soft-coated Wheaten Terrier crossed with the Bedlington Terrier, the Irish Terrier, and even the Irish Wolfhound. The blue, curly coat has attracted the legend that such a dog swam ashore and was considered so fine that he was mated to all the local wheaten-colored terriers; it is not impossible that there is some genetic influence from a Portuguese Water Dog on a visiting boat. The breed was a farm favorite, used for hunting vermin and otters, but only officially recognized in the late 19th century.

BREED QUALITIES

Today the breed is most likely to be found as a household dog, although it is still sometimes used for hunting. They can be time-consuming to groom, especially if the beard is left full, but make energetic, spirited companions.

YOUTHFUL COLOR Kerry Blues are born black and their coats gradually lighten as they mature. They can stay dark in color until they are fully grown, turning blue as late as two years old.

COAT CARE The wavy coat is soft and silky. Once it would have been allowed to form weatherproof cords, but it is now usually brushed every day or two and trimmed every six to ten weeks.

Manchester Terrier

ORIGIN United Kingdom
HEIGHT 15–16 in (38–41 cm)
WEIGHT 12–22 lb (5.5–10.0 kg)
EXERCISE LEVEL
COAT CARE
REGISTERED KC, FCI, AKCs
COLORS Black and tan

This breed name means something different on each side of the Atlantic. In the United Kingdom, it has one size, but in the United States there is a Toy version, similar to the English Toy Terrier.

BREED ORIGINS
Many of the British terrier breeds are descended from old black-and-tan types traceable back to the Middle Ages. The Manchester Terrier was created from this stock in the 19th century, and was the work of John Hulme. He crossed the terriers with Whippets for speed, and the resulting breed, excellent for ratting and rabbiting, was known for a time as "The Gentleman's Terrier." It is still a good outdoor companion, but is inclined to challenge other dogs and is too independent-minded to be a popular household dog.

EAR TYPES British dogs are shown with natural ears, but American dogs may still have them cropped. The end of cropping dented the breed's popularity in the United Kingdom.

Miniature Pinscher

ORIGIN Germany
HEIGHT 15–16 in (38–41 cm)
WEIGHT 12–22 lb (5.5–10.0 kg)
EXERCISE LEVEL
COAT CARE
REGISTERED KC, FCI, AKCs
COLORS Tan, black and tan; some allow blue or chocolate and tan

Also called the Zwergpinscher, this might look like a recent miniaturization of a working breed to make a toy companion, but in fact it has long been a compact working ratter.

 RED/TAN   BLACK AND TAN

BREED ORIGINS
This breed was developed from larger German Pinschers at least 500 years ago, but early dogs were tough ratters, since refined into a dog similar to the English Toy Terrier. It will pursue with relish, dig enthusiastically, and challenge dogs far larger than itself. It makes an effective watchdog and lively companion.

CHANGING FASHIONS American standards may still call for a docked tail and cropped ears, but European dogs are now shown undocked with either erect or dropped ears.

Parson Russell Terrier

ORIGIN United Kingdom
HEIGHT 11–15 in (28–38 cm)
WEIGHT 11–18 lb (5–8 kg)
EXERCISE LEVEL
COAT CARE
REGISTERED KC, FCI, AKCs
COLORS White and black or brown, tricolor

This breed is less popular in rural pursuits but has won wider recognition in show registries than the Jack Russell Terrier. The longer legs allowed dogs to keep up with mounted hunters.

BLACK AND WHITE

TAN AND WHITE

BLACK, WHITE AND TAN

BREED ORIGINS

This and its short-legged near-namesake were developed from white terriers used to pursue foxes underground. These went on to be recognized as Fox Terriers, but moved away from the working type, becoming too large to fit down earths. Reverend John "Jack" Russell developed his own fast and furious dogs from the same stock, and they remain closer to their roots. For a long time both types were classed together, but after much dispute, this breed is now recognized separately.

CHOICE OF COATS This breed has two versions, the wirehaired or broken coat seen here and preferred by Russell himself, and a sleeker smooth-haired type. Both are easy to care for and equally popular.

Scottish Terrier

ORIGIN United Kingdom
HEIGHT 10–11 in (25–28 cm)
WEIGHT 19–23 lb (8.6–10.5 kg)
EXERCISE LEVEL
COAT CARE
REGISTERED KC, FCI, AKCs
COLORS Black, wheaten, black brindle, red brindle

Once called the Aberdeen Terrier, and also generically called a Skye Terrier, the Scottie was nicknamed "Diehard" by the 19th-century Earl of Dumbarton, who had a famous pack of terriers.

BLACK

GOLD

BLACK BRINDLE

BREED ORIGINS

This breed is descended from terriers of the Scottish Western Isles, known as a type since the 16th century. It was developed in the 19th century, with all Scotties traceable back to one bitch, Splinter. They became hugely fashionable in the United States in the 1930s, possibly helped by President Roosevelt's pet, Fala;

George W. Bush's two Scotties have not worked similar magic. More companions than true terriers, they are loyal, stubborn, and spirited.

SCOTTIE LOOKS Instantly recognizable for its extravagant beard, the Scottie has an insulating double coat and may appreciate clipping or stripping in warmer climates. The ears are naturally pricked and quite narrow.

Skye Terrier

ORIGIN United Kingdom
HEIGHT 10 in (25 cm)
WEIGHT 19–25 lb (8.6–11.4 kg)
EXERCISE LEVEL
COAT CARE
REGISTERED KC, FCI, AKCs
COLORS Black, gray, fawn, cream

This breed is immortalized in Greyfriars Bobby, who is said to have spent 14 years sitting on the grave of his master in Greyfriars cemetery in Edinburgh until his own death.

BLACK   CREAM   GRAY   GOLD

BREED ORIGINS

Terriers on the Isle of Skye with hair covering their faces were described in the 16th century, but those could have resembled either this terrier or the Scottish Terrier, which was drawn from island stock. Their dwarf stature may have come from the same roots as the Swedish Vallhund or Welsh Corgis; there are also tales of a Spanish shipwreck and Maltese dogs coming ashore. The long coat, covering a graceful build, made it popular as a pet, but numbers have declined recently.

COAT CARE The long coat that is part of this breed's appeal is not very prone to matting, but it was kept clipped on working dogs.

UP OR DOWN? The ears of a Skye can be either pricked or dropped. Pricked ears are most common.

Smooth Fox Terrier

ORIGIN United Kingdom
HEIGHT 10–11 in (25–28 cm)
WEIGHT 15–22 lb (6.8–10.0 kg)
EXERCISE LEVEL
COAT CARE
REGISTERED KC, FCI, AKCs
COLORS White, white and tan, white and black, tricolor

The Smooth Fox Terrier is drawn from the same stock as the Jack and Parson Russell. This breed is now kept almost entirely as a companion, though not suited to city life.

BLACK AND WHITE   TAN AND WHITE   BLACK, WHITE AND TAN

BREED ORIGINS

A fox terrier was any dog that would drive foxes from their earths. This type was shown in the 1860s, and ancestors may include Beagles and even Bull Terriers. Although no longer a working dog, it is energetic and stubborn; it can be snappish, especially with younger children. A wire-coated variant was originally recognized alongside the smooth-coated version in many registries under the generic term "fox terrier," but the Wire Fox Terrier is now regarded as a separate breed.

SMOOTH FOX TERRIER
The back is strong and the chest is deep. The coat is straight and smooth.

Staffordshire Bull Terrier

ORIGIN United Kingdom
HEIGHT 14–16 in (36–41 cm)
WEIGHT 24–38 lb (10.9–17.3 kg)
EXERCISE LEVEL
COAT CARE
REGISTERED KC, FCI, AKCs
COLORS Any color except liver; solid or with white

The Staffie, although similar to some banned breeds, has so far not been subject to legislation in its homeland and most of Europe. It may look and walk like a thug, but it can be a pushover.

| BLACK | RED/TAN | GOLD AND WHITE | BLACK AND WHITE | BLACK BRINDLE |

BREED ORIGINS
This breed has its roots in dog-fighting, but the Staffie became a respectable recognized breed in the early 20th century. It is sweet-natured with humans but a ruthless fighter of any other dog. They are not recommended as solitary guards, because they should be well socialized; exercising them anywhere near other dogs is tricky.

FIGHTING FACE For dog fights, relatively long muzzles were needed, so short-faced bull baiters were crossed with terriers to produce the breed.

West Highland White Terrier

ORIGIN United Kingdom
HEIGHT 10–11 in (25–28 cm)
WEIGHT 15–22 lb (6.8–10.0 kg)
EXERCISE LEVEL
COAT CARE
REGISTERED KC, FCI, AKCs
COLORS White

A perennially popular breed, the Westie has been used as the face of dog food and, along with a black Scottish Terrier, Scotch whiskey. This dog is a bundle of fun that was created for a very sober reason.

BREED ORIGINS
The Westie is derived from white pups in wheaten Cairn Terrier litters. In the 19th century, these dogs flushed out game for guns, and were occasionally mistaken for prey and shot. So a white terrier that was easily distinguished from the quarry at any distance was developed; some credit the breed to Colonel E.D. Malcolm, others to the 8th Duke of Argyll. They are entertaining companions.

ITCHY COAT
Although the white coat saved the lives of working dogs, it had a price. White dogs are more susceptible than others to skin problems, and the Westie is particularly prone to allergies due to environmental factors or foods.

Yorkshire Terrier

ORIGIN United Kingdom
HEIGHT 9 in (23 cm)
WEIGHT 7 lb (3.2 kg)
EXERCISE LEVEL
COAT CARE
REGISTERED KC, FCI, AKCs
COLORS Steel-blue and tan

Although most registries now place the diminutive Yorkie in the toy or companion category, it was created as a ratter by miners and mill workers who never envisaged a bow in its hair. It remains a terrier at heart, and will challenge anything.

BREED ORIGINS

In the mid-19th century, Yorkshire was at the heart of the United Kingdom's industrial revolution. Many workers migrated to the area from Scotland, bringing their dogs with them. Clydesdale, Paisley, Skye, and Waterside and English Black-and-tan Terriers may have been involved in its ancestry. From this mix came a dog with an excess of spirit, valued for killing vermin. Today the breed is right at the top of the popularity stakes in the United States, but its size and spirit may be suffering from overexposure. Selective breeding for small size has led to slipped kneecaps and breathing problems in some lines.

EVERYDAY COAT The long, luxuriant, silvered coat takes time to develop. Pet owners usually find it easier to trim dogs back to a shorter length.

MINI DOGS Even the smallest Yorkies still produce the occasional pup larger than themselves. This is no bad thing: Breeding for ever-smaller dogs can lead to health problems.

Afghan Hound

ORIGIN Afghanistan
HEIGHT 25–29 in (64–74 cm)
WEIGHT 50–60 lb (22.5–27.5 kg)
EXERCISE LEVEL
COAT CARE
REGISTERED KC, FCI, AKCs
COLORS Any color, solid or shaded

The Afghan is perhaps the best known of the sighthounds. Originally at home in the harsh terrain and climate of the Afghan mountain ranges, it became a fashionable companion breed.

BLACK   CREAM   GRAY   GOLD   DARK BROWN

BREED ORIGINS

The Afghan is among the most ancient of all breeds. What is not clear is how thousands of years ago it came to the mountains of Afghanistan, far from the Arabian peninsula where dogs of this type originated. In its homeland, where it is still used for hunting, it is known as the Tazi, and a shorter-haired version exists; it is also called the Baluchi Hound. In the west, the longhaired version is an established companion breed,

prized for its aristocratic appearance and luxurious coat. These dogs lose their poised reserve when exercising and show their ancestors' speed and independence; sound obedience training is recommended if you want them to return to you. They are long lived for large dogs, reaching 12 to 14 years.

ANY COLOR YOU LIKE Although the golden coat is popular and seen as the "classic" Afghan look, any solid shade or combination is possible and allowed.

American Foxhound

ORIGIN United States
HEIGHT 21–25 in (53–64 cm)
WEIGHT 65–75 lb (29.4–34.0 kg)
EXERCISE LEVEL
COAT CARE
REGISTERED FCI, AKCs
COLORS Any color

Leaner and lighter than its European counterpart, the American Foxhound will act as an individual hunter or as a pack member, making it adaptable to a wider range of hunting styles.

GOLD AND WHITE   BLACK AND WHITE   TAN AND WHITE   BLACK AND TAN   BLACK, WHITE AND TAN

BREED ORIGINS

These dogs are descended from English hunting dogs brought to the United States in the 1860s. Irish and French hounds were added to the mix, taking the breed in a slightly different direction. Today, show lines also find a place as good-natured companions. They are loyal to their family and good with children, but like all hunting dogs are not trustworthy around other noncanine pets. They are a fairly healthy breed, usually living over a decade.

WORKING DOGS When seeking a family companion, choose show bloodlines. Dogs that are bred for working do not make good pets.

Basenji

ORIGIN Zaire
HEIGHT 16–17 in (41–43 cm)
WEIGHT 21–24 lb (9.5–11.0 kg)
EXERCISE LEVEL
COAT CARE
REGISTERED KC, FCI, AKCs
COLORS Black and white, tan and white, black, or brindle

This dog resembles those depicted in tomb paintings from ancient Egypt, and has primitive characteristics, such as a tendency to howl rather than bark, that seem to show it is an ancient breed.

BLACK   BLACK AND WHITE   TAN AND WHITE

BREED ORIGINS
The story of the Basenji breed today begins in the 1930s with dogs brought from Africa to Europe and originally called Congo Dogs. They are not easily trained, but are reliable with children. Although long lived, they are prone to an inheritable disorder of the kidneys.

NO WORRIES A wrinkled face gives this affectionate, intelligent, and energetic breed a misleadingly anxious look.

PRIMITIVE LOOKS These small dogs are muscular and powerful. The tail is typically carried in a curl over the rump.

Basset Hound

ORIGIN United Kingdom
HEIGHT 13–14 in (33–36 cm)
WEIGHT 40–60 lb (18.1–27.2 kg)
EXERCISE LEVEL
COAT CARE
REGISTERED KC, FCI, AKCs
COLORS Any hound color

The best known of all the bassets, this breed has lost any geographical qualification of its name. The exact location of its origin is hazy, but it is regarded as a classically British breed.

GOLD AND WHITE   TAN AND WHITE   BLACK, WHITE, AND TAN

BREED ORIGINS
The Basset is descended from dwarfed bloodhounds, and dates back to at least the 1500s. The first breed description may be Theseus's account of his hounds in Shakespeare's *A Midsummer Night's Dream*: "With ears that sweep away the morning dew/Crook-kneed, and dewlapped like Thessalian bulls/Slow in pursuit, but matched in mouth like bells."

Today the Basset is more often a household dog than a hunting companion. This is an affectionate, amenable breed, good with children. It can be easily distracted, so needs consistent, patient training.

BULKY BUILD The short, crooked legs make the Basset slow, but it should never be clumsy. Lighter types are still used in hunting work, more in the United States than in Europe.

Beagle

ORIGIN United Kingdom
HEIGHT 13–15 in (33–39 cm)
WEIGHT 18–30 lb (8.2–13.6 kg)
EXERCISE LEVEL
COAT CARE
REGISTERED KC, FCI, AKCs
COLORS Any hound color

The Beagle is most often described in breed standards as a "merry" hound. It has a bell-like baying voice and a lively, curious personality, and can make an excellent family dog.

GOLD AND
WHITE

BLACK, WHITE,
AND TAN

BREED ORIGINS

The Beagle probably derives from the larger Harrier breed, and has been used for hunting in Britain since the Middle Ages. These small dogs could even be carried by mounted hunters in saddlebags, and were bred to pursue rabbits and birds, either in packs or solo. Today, the breed varies in size from place to place, but has a distinct personality.

ENDEARING LOOKS
The affectionate nature of the Beagle is advertised in its typically appealing expression, but with the exception of Snoopy they are not to be trusted around small animals such as birds.

BEAGLE BODY The Beagle resembles a small Foxhound. It has a sturdy build, with a tail carried high or "gaily," and a short, sleek coat that is easy to care for.

BREED QUALITIES

Beagles are highly sociable, and crave company, either human or canine. If they are to be left alone at all, keep at least two. They may pine alone, and a howling Beagle will make no friends among neighbors.

In the right home, Beagles can be a delight: Cheerful, affectionate dogs that are not aggressive, they are good with children and friendly with other dogs. They are not the easiest to train, however, and tend to follow their own noses when out and about.

Black-and-Tan Coonhound

ORIGIN United States
HEIGHT 23–27 in (58–69 cm)
WEIGHT 55–75 lb (24.9–34.0 kg)
EXERCISE LEVEL
COAT CARE
REGISTERED FCI, AKCs
COLORS Black and tan

Coonhounds are a specialized group of hunting dogs, bred to track and "tree" the raccoon or oppossum and then await the hunter's arrival. They hunt by scent, and have a distinctive baying call.

POWER HOUND This large hound has a strong, well-proportioned build, with a deep chest and a strong tail. Long legs and a rhythmic stride give it speed.

BREED ORIGINS

The Black-and-Tan Coonhound was developed in the 18th century in the United States, although it was not officially recognized until 1945. It was created by crossing Bloodhounds and Foxhounds, and the Kerry Beagle may also have contributed to its development. The Coonhound howls as it works, and the following hunter can tell from the sound when the quarry has been treed.

Although intended for hunting raccoons, the breed is a versatile and capable hunter and has also been used very successfully to hunt larger game such as deer and even mountain lion and bears. This is the best known of all the coonhound breeds, and popular for its trainable temperament. It can make a good watchdog, and is an asset to homes that can provide plenty of exercise and interest.

COONHOUND HEAD The head is finely modeled, with no folds in the skin. The ears are set low and well back, hanging in graceful folds; they should reach past the end of the nose.

PRACTICAL COAT The short, sleek coat is largely coal black with rich tan markings confined to the muzzle, limbs, and chest. The insulating coat withstands extremes of both heat and cold well.

Bloodhound

ORIGIN Belgium
HEIGHT 23–27 in (58–69 cm)
WEIGHT 66–110 lb (30.0–50.0 kg)
EXERCISE LEVEL
COAT CARE
REGISTERED KC, FCI, AKCs
COLORS Black and tan, liver/red and tan, red

Developed in Belgium as the Chien de St. Hubert and in England as the Bloodhound, this massive scenthound is synonymous with tracking, and has been used to trace criminals and runaway slaves.

RED/TAN

BLACK AND TAN

BREED ORIGINS

This droopy breed is said to be directly descended from the packs of hounds belonging to St. Hubert, patron saint of hunters, in the 7th century. These dogs were maintained for centuries by Benedictine monks at the Abbaye de Saint-Hubert in the Ardennes, and by tradition six dogs were sent every year to the king of France for the royal packs. Taken to Britain by the Normans, the same lines became known as the Bloodhound, referring not to an ability to scent blood, but to a dog of "pure" blood, belonging to the nobility.

BREED QUALITIES

A gentle, affectionate breed, the Bloodhound needs to be watched around children only because it may bowl them over. It is too easily distracted by interesting scents to be highly trainable, and knows how to use those mournful eyes. Sadly, it can be short lived and is one of the breeds most prone to bloat; joint problems and cancers are also issues, as in most large breeds.

CLASSIC LOOKS Although Bloodhounds now come in a limited range of shades, there was once a wider selection. It included a white strain, known as the Talbot Hound, which had died out by the 17th century.

Borzoi

ORIGIN Russia

HEIGHT 27–31 in (69–79 cm)

WEIGHT 75–105 lb (34.0–47.6 kg)

EXERCISE LEVEL

COAT CARE

REGISTERED KC, FCI, AKCs

COLORS White, golden, tan, or gray with black markings, either solid or mixed

This elegant and reserved dog comes from a heritage of hunting wolves in Russia, and has also been called the Russian Wolfhound. In the last century, it has moved successfully from hunt to home.

CREAM

GOLD

GOLD AND WHITE

BLACK AND WHITE

TAN AND WHITE

BREED ORIGINS

Sighthounds had arrived in Russia from their original home in southwestern Asia by the Middle Ages. Here, they developed into the Borzoi, a Russian term for all sighthounds, including some rarities virtually unknown in the West, such as the Taigan and Chortaj. The Borzoi had spread westward into Europe by the 19th century, where it became favored as a high-status pet and an aristocratic household dog, and was bred for companionship rather than hunting.

Today it is widely known as a household pet, but it has retained all its ancestors' athleticism and free spirit. It remains a hunter at heart, and cannot be trusted to resist the urge to hunt any small animal, so will not live peacefully with noncanine pets. Although this breed needs plenty of exercise, it quickly wearies of very young children's rough and tumble play, and prefers an ordered life.

NOBLE NOSE The head is distinctively long and narrow, with a slightly arched muzzle and ears that lie back on the neck when relaxed.

COAT CARE The silky coat presents a challenge when shed for the summer, but is otherwise not that hard to care for. Brush regularly and clip hair between the toes.

FAST MOVER Like all sighthounds, the Borzoi is capable of amazing feats of speed, and is easily distracted while out and about. Constant vigilance is needed when exercising these dogs.

Dachshunds

ORIGIN Germany
HEIGHT 7–9 in (18–23 cm)
WEIGHT 15–25 lb (6.8–11.3 kg)
EXERCISE LEVEL
COAT CARE
REGISTERED KC, FCI, AKCs
COLORS One color, bicolor, or dappled or striped; no white

This breed group has a complex set of categories according to both size and coat type that differ from country to country. Dogs bred for working differ from those that are bred for showing.

CREAM

BLUE

RED/TAN

GOLD

BLACK AND TAN

BREED ORIGINS

Dwarfed or short-legged dogs have been known for thousands of years, and the Dachshund, also called the Dackel or Teckel in Europe, has been known as a type since the Middle Ages. Bred from the hunting dogs known as Bracken, they were selected because their short stature made them suitable for working underground, hence their name, which means "badger dog."

Today, these dogs are kept both as hunting companions and household pets. Those bred for working have shorter spines and longer legs than those bred for showing; the latter are more prone to spine problems, always a risk with this build.

FULL OF POTENTIAL The different sizes of Dachshunds are not distinct breeds, so what a puppy may be is always open to chance, although lines tend to produce certain sizes consistently.

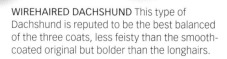

WIREHAIRED DACHSHUND This type of Dachshund is reputed to be the best balanced of the three coats, less feisty than the smooth-coated original but bolder than the longhairs.

BREED DIFFERENCES

As well as the various sizes of Dachshunds (*see* box), there are three different coats: The Smooth-haired, the Wirehaired, and the Longhaired. The Smooth-haired is the oldest, the original hunting dog. The Wirehaired was created by crossing with rough-haired Pinschers, and using the Dandie Dinmont Terrier to improve the head type. The Longhaired is thought to come from crosses with short-legged spaniels, with further work to miniaturize the resulting dogs. The differences are more than cosmetic: all of these crosses also affected the temperament.

BREED QUALITIES

Although it is a small dog that can adapt to urban life, needing little space for exercise, some caution is needed when choosing this popular breed. They are variable in temper, and some seem to have the will of a much larger dog in concentrated form. Be prepared to give firm and

SMOOTH-HAIRED DACHSHUND The original coat, this shorthaired type is the most excitable. They can be fearful and snappish.

consistent training when they are young or face a lifetime of challenge—and these robust small dogs often live on into their mid- to late teens.

LONGHAIRED DACHSHUND Spaniel heritage has given this breed not only a silky coat but a tendency to be much less tenacious than their Smooth-haired cousins, and even rather shy.

Sizes of Dachshund

British and American clubs tend to recognize two sizes of Dachshund, the Standard and the Miniature, with the dividing line between the two set at 11 lb (5 kg). Continental European clubs classify by chest circumference—a vital statistic for an earth dog. Dachshunds have a chest of 14 in (35 cm), Miniatures 12–14 in (30–35 cm), and Rabbit Dachshunds or Kaninchen Teckel below 12 in (30 cm).

Deerhound

ORIGIN United Kingdom
HEIGHT 28–30 in (71–76 cm)
WEIGHT 80–100 lb (36.3–45.4 kg)
EXERCISE LEVEL
COAT CARE
REGISTERED KC, FCI, AKCs
COLORS Gray, brindle, yellow, sandy-red, or red fawn with black points; some white allowed

Historically Scottish, this is also called the Scottish Deerhound. Its original purpose was hunting deer, but it is now most often a gentle, friendly, and undeniably impressive companion.

GRAY   RED/TAN   GOLD   BLACK BRINDLE

BREED ORIGINS

Rough-coated hounds have been recorded for over 500 years, probably descended from ancient imported short-coated sighthounds crossed with longer-coated dogs suited to the Scottish Highlands' climate. Packs hunted deer, but with the demise of the clan system and the shift to hunting with guns, the breed declined by the 18th century. It was revived in the 19th century, but remains rare.

This is an intelligent and trainable hound, sociable with both children and other dogs. It does not need a large home, since adults are layabouts indoors, but a good-sized outdoor space and thorough daily exercise are vital.

DEERHOUND LOOKS Everything from the head to the tail has a long, strong, tapering line. The coat is shaggy, never wooly, and much softer on the head, chest, and stomach than elsewhere.

Drever

ORIGIN Sweden
HEIGHT 12–16 in (30–41 cm)
WEIGHT 30–33 lb (13.6–15.0 kg)
EXERCISE LEVEL
COAT CARE
REGISTERED FCI
COLORS Fawn and white, black and white, tricolor

Also called the Swedish Dachsbracke, this accomplished scenthound is among the most popular hunting dogs in its homeland. It is used to track and drive quarry toward the hunters.

GOLD AND WHITE   BLACK AND WHITE   BLACK, WHITE, AND TAN

SLOW BUT STEADY Short legs mean this is not the fastest of hounds, but it has incredible stamina and a tenacious desire to hunt.

BREED ORIGINS

This is a recreation of a historic type, bred from the Westphalian Dachsbracke crossed with local hounds. Its compact size makes it suited to slowly driving flighty deer toward guns, and this hardy, robust breed is a tenacious hunter. When hunting is not available, these dogs make laid-back, amenable companions, although they are self-contained and not the ideal family dog.

TIDY FACE The Drever head is large, but well proportioned. Unlike some other hounds, it has close-fitting eyelids and lips, rather than droopy folds.

English Coonhound

ORIGIN United States

HEIGHT 21–27 in (53–69 cm)

WEIGHT 40–65 lb (18.1–29.5 kg)

EXERCISE LEVEL

COAT CARE

REGISTERED AKCs

COLORS Any hound color; most often red tick

Despite its misleading name, this robust scenthound is an entirely American breed. It was first bred for hunting raccoons and similar quarry, a role that it still fulfills today, mostly in the southern states.

BLUE | RED/TAN | BLACK AND WHITE | TAN AND WHITE | BLACK, WHITE AND TAN

BUILD AND COAT This is a relatively small coonhound, but powerful and strong boned. It slopes from the shoulders to the rump, but the long ears and drooping lips are typical of the type.

BREED ORIGINS
This breed is also sometimes called the Redtick Coonhound, a name perhaps more suitable, since its ancestors included not only English but French dogs, bred in the early 19th century.

This is first and foremost a hunting dog, robust and active with high energy levels. It does make a good-tempered household and family companion, as long as there are no small, noncanine pets to consider.

Finnish Hound

ORIGIN Finland

HEIGHT 22–25 in (56–63 cm)

WEIGHT 44–55 lb (20.0–25.0 kg)

EXERCISE LEVEL

COAT CARE

REGISTERED FCI, AKCs

COLORS Tricolor

The Suomenjokoira or Finsk Stovåre is a versatile tracker used for tracking hare and fox by scent. A medium-sized breed with a resonant voice, it is the most popular of Finland's working dogs.

BREED ORIGINS
Some accounts say this Harrier-like breed dates from the 18th century and was created by a goldsmith named Tammelin using Swedish, German, and French hounds. The official standard, however, dates its origins not further back than the 1890s, after the creation of the Finnish Kennel Club, and merely mentions Finnish dogs that resembled European breeds. However it began, it is an enthusiastic hunter that brings prey to bay for the hunter; it will also find shot birds, but does not retrieve.

KEEN NOSE This indefatigable hound will relish hunting in all conditions. It works independently, tracking the quarry and bringing it to bay.

Greyhound

ORIGIN United Kingdom
HEIGHT 27–30 in (69–76 cm)
WEIGHT 60–70 lb (27.2–31.7 kg)
EXERCISE LEVEL
COAT CARE
REGISTERED KC, FCI, AKCs
COLORS Black, white, red, blue, fawn, fallow, or brindle, with or without white

There are Italian, Hungarian, Russian, and other Greyhounds, and this member of the group is also known as the English Greyhound. Closely resembling dogs in ancient art, it is renowned for its speed.

BLACK   BLUE   RED/TAN   GOLD   BLACK AND WHITE

BREED ORIGINS

Ancient Egyptian art shows dogs similar to the modern Greyhound, and is seized upon as evidence of the breed's antiquity. However, DNA analysis in 2004 put it surprisingly close to herding dogs, implying that while this deep-chested, narrow-waisted, finely tapered type of dog has been around for millennia, the modern breed sprang from a wider genetic base more recently.

The "grey" does not refer to color, but comes from Old English, and is thought to mean "fine." Greyhounds were used in hunting large and small game, and today are principally used in racing.

BREED QUALITIES

Despite their speed in pursuit, the Greyhound at home can be a relaxed and relaxing companion, although not ideal for city life and families with young children. It tends to forget its training when it sights potential prey, but is otherwise tractable.

BUILT FOR SPEED Greyhounds can reach speeds of 43 mph (69 kph); retired racing dogs can find it hard to break the habits of a lifetime when they see small animals.

LIVE FAST, RETIRE YOUNG Racing dogs have a short working life, and rescue organizations often have adult dogs to home. Away from the track, the Greyhound is typically quiet and gentle.

Irish Wolfhound

ORIGIN Ireland

HEIGHT 32–34 in (81–86 cm)

WEIGHT 105–120 lb (47.6–54.4 kg)

EXERCISE LEVEL

COAT CARE

REGISTERED KC, FCI, AKCs

COLORS Gray, steel-gray, brindle, red, black, pure white, fawn, wheaten

This massive breed makes it easy to imagine the fearsome Celtic hounds known as Cú Faoil used for hunting wolves, elk, and boar, and partly responsible for the local extinction of all three.

GRAY

RED/TAN

SHAGGY DOG The coarse, wiry top coat is best stripped out by plucking in summer, leaving a sleek, soft undercoat for the warmer months.

THE EYES HAVE IT For all its size and power, this is the original gentle giant, most likely to lick you to death.

BREED ORIGINS

The ancestors of this hound probably came to Ireland via the Roman Empire, and large, shaggy hounds are prominent in ancient Irish writing. By the 19th century numbers were seriously depleted; this is not a dog suited to hunting with a gun.

The breed was saved by a Captain Graham, who used Deerhound, Great Dane, and Borzoi lines to inject new blood.

Today, the breed is a mellow household companion, good with children and other dogs and perhaps less inclined to chase than some other sighthounds. Sadly, it is not long lived, and is prone to bone cancer and gastric torsion, like other giant and deep-chested breeds.

Saluki

ORIGIN Iran
HEIGHT 20–28 in (51–71 cm)
WEIGHT 44–66 lb (20.0–29.9 kg)
EXERCISE LEVEL
COAT CARE
REGISTERED KC, FCI, AKCs
COLORS Any color or colors except brindle

Also called the Arabian Greyhound, Persian Greyhound, or Gazelle Hound, this swift and elegant sighthound has been known in the Middle East and used in the hunt for millennia.

BLACK GOLD GOLD AND WHITE

BREED ORIGINS

The Saluki closely resembles ancient images of hunting dogs, and recent DNA analysis confirmed that it is not a modern recreation but a truly ancient breed. It predates Islam, and while dogs are generally regarded as unclean in the religion, the Saluki was always an exception; the white spot often found on its chest is known as "the kiss of Allah" by the Bedouin. It

was first brought to the United Kingdom in the 1840s, but only became popular at the start of the 20th century. Today it is established across the world as a graceful companion, at ease in family and city homes.

NATURAL VARIATION Because the breed was historically scattered across a wide area, a range of geographically isolated local types emerged. The coat varies in color between places, and both smooth and feathered types exist.

Sloughi

ORIGIN Morocco
HEIGHT 24–28 in (60–70 cm)
WEIGHT 44–59 lb (20.0–27.0 kg)
EXERCISE LEVEL
COAT CARE
REGISTERED KC, FCI, AKCs
COLORS Sand to fawn, may have black shading or white markings

Although it is sometimes called the Arabian Greyhound and classed with the Saluki, recent DNA analysis has shown the Sloughi to be a distinctively African breed.

GOLD GOLD AND WHITE

BREED ORIGINS

When looking at the relationships between animals, a mixture of archeology, written records, and the looks of the breed have in the past been the only tools available. Beyond a certain distance, these can give no great certainty. The advent of genetic studies has shone a new light on the history of dog breeds, and revealed some surprises. Although it looks close to the other breeds sometimes called greyhounds, the

Sloughi appears to have spent all of its genetic history in Africa, almost entirely untouched by any new input. It has needed none: A slender, sand-colored dog, it is in many ways the perfect hound for its home. A slightly high-strung breed and suspicious of strangers, it is content as the companion of a consistent, quiet owner but not a choice for a rowdy household with children.

HAPPY MEDIUM The Berbers kept two lines of Sloughis: The small, fine desert Sloughi, and a larger mountain Sloughi. Elsewhere, the breed has developed as a blend of the two.

Swedish Elkhound

ORIGIN Sweden

HEIGHT 23–25 in (58–64 cm)

WEIGHT 66 lb (29.9 kg)

EXERCISE LEVEL

COAT CARE

REGISTERED FCI

COLORS Shades of gray with cream to white markings

The official national breed of Sweden, this dog is also known by the name of Jämthund. Once there were many more regional elkhounds, and this one originated in Jämtland in northern Sweden.

BREED ORIGINS

This dog dates back many centuries, and was traditionally used for hunting not only elk but bears, wolves, and even the agile Scandinavian lynx, driving the quarry until it was trapped and then awaiting the hunters' arrival. It was only recognized in the latter part of the 20th century; until then it was judged as part of the Norwegian Elkhound breed, a politically unpopular union. In truth, many physically isolated communities developed their own slightly different strains of hunting dog over the centuries; this one simply survived and got itself noticed. This heritage has created a strong, hardy dog of enormous stamina. It is also intelligent, and has proved adaptable.

WORKING ANIMAL The wolf-like appearance identifies this as a breed that is happiest when it has a job to do.

Whippet

ORIGIN United Kingdom

HEIGHT 17–20 in (43–51 cm)

WEIGHT 28 lb (12.7 kg)

EXERCISE LEVEL

COAT CARE

REGISTERED KC, FCI, AKCs

COLORS Any color

This Greyhound in miniature is one of the fastest sighthounds in existence. Both its official name and the nickname "snap dog" are said to refer to it moving as fast as a snapped or cracked whip.

BLACK   CREAM   BLUE   RED/TAN

BREED ORIGINS

The Whippet was created in the north of England in the 19th century. Hare coursing was a popular sport, and crossing Fox Terriers with the Greyhound—which was too large for the sport—created the Whippet. Despite its graceful, slight appearance, this is a hardy hunter, with all the tenacity of its terrier antecedents when on a scent. At home, this is a gentle, affectionate breed, relaxed around children and other dogs and even something of a couch potato, especially in winter.

TAKE COVER Thin skin and a fine, close coat provide little protection or insulation. A jacket in cold weather is practical, not a fashion statement.

American Cocker Spaniel

ORIGIN United States

HEIGHT 14–15 in (36–38 cm)

WEIGHT 24–28 lb (10.9–12.7 kg)

EXERCISE LEVEL

COAT CARE

REGISTERED KC, FCI, AKCs

COLORS Black, cream, red, brown; solid or with white; tan points

In the United States this breed is simply the Cocker Spaniel, and the original type is known as the English Cocker Spaniel, but international registries give each their national identity.

BLACK | RED/TAN | GOLD | GOLD AND WHITE | BLACK AND WHITE

BREED ORIGINS

This breed has the same early history as the English Cocker, but American breeders pursued a prettier dog, with longer, silkier hair, rather than working qualities. In 1936 a group broke away and formed an "English Cocker Spaniel" club. Some solid

colors may suffer "avalanche of rage" syndrome, but otherwise these are affectionate, gentle companions, rarely seen as working dogs.

BEAUTY REGIME The dense coat is prone to dry or oily seborrhea, and hair on the ears must be trimmed to let air reach the ear canals, minimizing infections. The hairy feet are magnets for debris.

Brittany

ORIGIN France

HEIGHT 19–20 in (48–51 cm)

WEIGHT 35–40 lb (15.9–18.1 kg)

EXERCISE LEVEL

COAT CARE

REGISTERED KC, FCI, AKCs

COLORS Black and white, orange and white, liver and white, tricolor

A favorite gundog in France, this breed is also popular abroad. Although it is known as the Epagneul Breton in its homeland, elsewhere the "spaniel" is usually omitted; it is more of a setter.

BLACK AND WHITE | TAN AND WHITE | BLACK, WHITE, AND TAN

BREED ORIGINS

One of the oldest breeds of this type in France, this was almost extinct at the start of the 20th century, when it was revived by breeder Arthur Enaud through outcrossing and renewed selections. Its popularity is as much due to its relaxed tolerance of children and other dogs as its working abilities, and this is an obedient, affectionate companion for anyone who can provide sufficient activity.

TRUE COLORS In the United States, only brown and red shades, seen as "classic" French colors, are allowed. In Europe, black is also allowed, since it was in the original French breed standard that was drawn up in 1907.

English Cocker Spaniel

ORIGIN United Kingdom
HEIGHT 15–17 in (38–43 cm)
WEIGHT 26–34 lb (11.8–15.4 kg)
EXERCISE LEVEL
COAT CARE
REGISTERED KC, FCI, AKCs
COLORS Black, cream, red, brown, solid or with white, tan points

In the United Kingdom, this breed is simply the Cocker Spaniel, but elsewhere its nationality is added to distinguish it from the American Cocker Spaniel. Side by side, nobody could mistake the two today.

BLACK   RED/TAN   GOLD   GOLD AND WHITE   BLACK AND WHITE

BREED ORIGINS

Spaniels were used to flush game into nets as early as the 16th century. Cockers, specializing in woodcock, were described in the 19th century. These dogs are now the second most popular breed in their homeland, and show and working lines have diverged. Working dogs are smaller, with shorter coats, and boundless energy, while show dogs need more coat care but less mental and physical stimulation.

COLOR AND TEMPERAMENT A rare condition called "avalanche of rage" syndrome can affect solid-colored, but not bicolored, dogs.

English Pointer

ORIGIN United Kingdom
HEIGHT 21–24 in (53–61 cm)
WEIGHT 44–66 lb (20.0–29.9 kg)
EXERCISE LEVEL
COAT CARE
REGISTERED KC, FCI, AKCs
COLORS White and black, liver, lemon, or orange

Many registries officially list this aristocratic-looking dog simply as the Pointer, but given the number of pointing breeds in the world, it is widely given its national identity for the sake of clarity.

GOLD AND WHITE   BLACK AND WHITE   TAN AND WHITE

BREED ORIGINS

It is thought that Greyhounds, Bloodhounds, setters, foxhounds, and even bulldog breeds contributed to their development. Pointers are recorded in England as far back as 1650, but continental breeds such as the Spanish Pointer were involved in their creation. By the 18th century these were perhaps the most popular hunting dog, and became popular in the United States by the 1900s.

A fast and reliable scenter that can quickly cover a wide area, the English Pointer is especially adept at finding feathered game, and is used for hunting and in competitive trials, in which they excel. As companions, they are serious and sensitive but they are also biddable and gentle.

English Setter

ORIGIN United Kingdom
HEIGHT 24–25 in (61–64 cm)
WEIGHT 40–70 lb (18.1–31.8 kg)
EXERCISE LEVEL
COAT CARE
REGISTERED KC, FCI, AKCs
COLORS White and black, orange, lemon, or liver, tricolor

This elegant breed combines old-fashioned looks with old-fashioned manners. It is a proficient tracker, setter, and retriever of birds, but just as happy as an active family dog, and a peaceful companion.

GOLD AND WHITE

BLACK AND WHITE

TAN AND WHITE

BREED ORIGINS
The first setters were developed in France from Spanish and French spaniels, and were in England by the 16th century, but the modern breed was developed by Sir Edward Laverack in the 19th century. It is now split into the show lines and the often lighter-built working or field lines, which include the strain known as Llewellin Setters.

BREED LOOKS Like all the British setter breeds, the English has a feathery coat that comes in its own distinctive pattern, an all-over fleck that is known as "belton" by breeders.

English Springer Spaniel

ORIGIN United Kingdom
HEIGHT 19–20 in (48–51 cm)
WEIGHT 49–55 lb (22.2–24.9 kg)
EXERCISE LEVEL
COAT CARE
REGISTERED KC, FCI, AKCs
COLORS Liver and white, black and white, tricolor

One of the oldest surviving spaniel breeds, this is still a popular working dog and household companion in the United Kingdom, and also among the top breeds registered in showing circles.

BLACK AND WHITE

BLACK, WHITE, AND TAN

BREED ORIGINS
Dogs of this type can be seen in paintings from the 17th century, but were then simply spaniels, not springers, used on furred game, and cockers, used for birds. In fact, this breed has been shown by American hunters to be a proficient bird dog. It is strongly split into working and show lines, but show lines still need exercise and stimulation, or, for all their gentleness, they may become destructive.

SHOW AND FIELD This is a show type dog, with pendulous ears and lips, and a long coat that is mainly colored. Field types are lighter and more wiry with a fairly short, feathery coat, predominantly white for visibility.

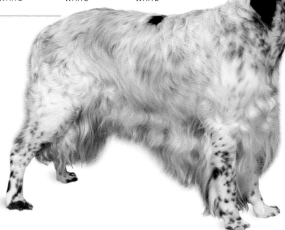

French Spaniel

ORIGIN France

HEIGHT 22–24 in (55–61 cm)

WEIGHT 44–55 lb (20.0–25.0 kg)

EXERCISE LEVEL

COAT CARE

REGISTERED FCI, AKCs

COLORS White and brown, from cinnamon to dark liver

This breed is known as the Epagneul Français in its homeland, where it is also patriotically claimed by its admirers to be the origin of all the diverse varieties of hunting spaniels.

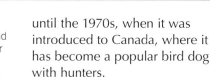

FRENCH COAT The coat is generally flat and silky, softened by longer feathering on the ears, legs, and tail, usually seen with medium brown spotting.

As with other French breeds, it lost out in favor of British breeds in the 19th century and was on the verge of extinction, but it was rescued by a priest, Father Fournier. The breed remained almost unknown outside France until the 1970s, when it was introduced to Canada, where it has become a popular bird dog with hunters.

BREED QUALITIES

Rustic in looks, this is an ideal country dog that will encourage long walks, but it is calm indoors and rarely barks, so can adapt to city life too. It is gentle and obedient, and like most of the French gundogs has a sensitive temperament that craves affection and needs soft words to give its best.

BREED ORIGINS

Despite its name, this old breed, which dates back to the 17th century, is more of a pointer or setter than a spaniel. Early dogs of this type would set or point very low, so a hunter behind them could throw a net over them onto the game ahead. As hunting methods changed, the higher pointing style was developed, and this breed is still a fine pointer and retriever. It is also good for flushing game in water and over wild, rugged terrain, although it is not the fastest of spaniels.

SIMILAR FEATURES This breed is thought to be related to the Small Munsterlander and the Dutch Partridge Dog. While conventional thought has it that this type of dog spread from Spain to France and beyond, some believe that it is fundamentally Danish.

German Pointers

ORIGIN Germany

HEIGHT 23–26 in (59–66 cm)

WEIGHT 55–70 lb (24.9–31.8 kg)

EXERCISE LEVEL

COAT CARE ⟋ (sh) ⟍ (lh)

REGISTERED KC, FCI, AKCs

COLORS Black, brown; solid or with white in variable mixes of specks and patches

There are three types of this versatile hunting dog: The Kurzhaar (Shorthaired), Drahthaar (Wirehaired) and Stichelhaar (Longhaired). It will retrieve as well as point, and works in all kinds of terrain.

BLACK   DARK BROWN   BLACK AND WHITE   TAN AND WHITE

BREED ORIGINS

The ancestry of the German Pointer goes back to pointers that came to Germany from Spain and France. Once sophisticated shotguns were in use, bringing down distant birds in flight, these specialized dogs needed to expand their repertoire to include retrieving. Intensely focused breeding activity in Germany in the late 19th century saw British and French breeds mixed with the national stock to create a versatile and tireless hunting dog. The result of this was the range of German Pointers, of which the Shorthaired is the most successful. They are popular hunting dogs, with the intelligence to work independently.

SHORTHAIRED The coat may be patched, flecked, or both. Conformation and constitution are more important: A dog must be able to carry out any and all hunting activities.

BREED QUALITIES

Like most gundog breeds, these are loyal and affectionate dogs, gentle to handle and devoted to their family; German Pointers have always been household as well as hunting dogs. But they are powerful, with limitless energy, and need as much exercise as possible. If neglected, they can be destructive or hyperactive, and they may become ardent escape artists.

SOFT MOUTH Because this breed retrieves as well as points, the muzzle must be long, broad, deep, and strong so that the dog can carry game gently without damaging it.

WIREHAIRED The wiry coat is quite water repellent making this the most weather resistant of the German pointers. The Longhaired, or Stichelhaar, is seen far less than the other two.

Golden Retriever

ORIGIN United Kingdom
HEIGHT 22–24 in (56–61 cm)
WEIGHT 60–75 lb (27.2–34.0 kg)
EXERCISE LEVEL
COAT CARE
REGISTERED KC, FCI, AKCs
COLORS Gold

Having ruled the popularity stakes for years, the gregarious and genial Golden Retriever has begun to decline in numbers. It may be fashion, lifestyles making them harder to accommodate, or simply "too much of a good thing" turning sour.

BREED ORIGINS

Developed in Scotland from the 1860s by Sir Dudley Majoribanks, Goldens started with Nous, a yellow puppy from a litter of black retrievers, and Belle, from the now extinct Tweed Water Spaniel breed. The results were first shown in 1906 as "any other color" retrievers, and became a breed within a few years: Recognition in North America came in the 1920s and 1930s. As with other highly popular dogs, overbreeding of this friendly, "live-to-please" breed has led to health and temperament problems in some lines.

BIGGER AND BETTER
Improvements in guns in the 19th century meant a powerful retriever was needed to bring back birds downed over long distances, and the Golden fulfilled this role.

COLOR COUNTS There are different lines of Goldens for field trials, working, assistance dogs, and showing. In the show lines, American dogs are darker than British dogs.

Gordon Setter

ORIGIN United Kingdom
HEIGHT 23–27 in (58–69 cm)
WEIGHT 45–80 lb (20.4–36.2 kg)
EXERCISE LEVEL
COAT CARE
REGISTERED KC, FCI, AKCs
COLORS Black and tan

This black-and-tan setter is a tireless runner, bred to cover great tracts of the Scottish Highlands in pursuit of grouse, ptarmigan, and partridge. Less often seen as a working dog than in the past, it makes an ebullient companion.

CHANGING LOOKS Although black-and-tan setters were known in England and Scotland in the 16th century, this breed was originally a tricolor; white is now limited to small markings.

BREED ORIGINS
Setters find birds that freeze to escape notice, and then similarly freeze: Falcons or a thrown net accomplish the rest. This breed was developed by the Duke of Richmond and Gordon in Scotland in the early 19th century. Better guns and a decline in partridge in the 20th century made retrievers more useful, so this is usually a household companion today. Loyal and obedient, they can be bouncy.

Hungarian Vizsla

ORIGIN Hungary
HEIGHT 22–24 in (56–61 cm)
WEIGHT 49–62 lb (22.2–28.1 kg)
EXERCISE LEVEL
COAT CARE
REGISTERED KC, FCI, AKCs
COLORS Chestnut-gold

This breed is called simply the Visla in the United States, and the Hungarian Shorthaired Pointer or Rövidszörü Magyar Vizsla in Europe. It is now popular both at home and abroad.

BREED ORIGINS
Pointers working with falcons were recorded in the 14th-century "Vienna Chronicle" of Hungarian codes and laws. At first called the Yellow Pointer, it became the Hungarian Pointer, and by the 16th century the Vizsla, a name that may come from an old Hungarian word meaning "search." An influx of English and German pointers in the 19th century almost made the breed extinct, as did World War II, but today it is popular at home and abroad, and has given rise to the Hungarian Wirehaired Vizsla.

LOOKS FAMILIAR The Vizsla was used in development of other breeds of similar lines, most notably the German Shorthaired Pointer and the Weimaraner; in turn, these same breeds may have been among the dogs used to re-establish the Vizsla after numbers fell in the 19th century.

Hungarian Wirehaired Vizsla

ORIGIN Hungary
HEIGHT 22–24 in (56–61 cm)
WEIGHT 49–62 lb (22.2–28.1 kg)
EXERCISE LEVEL
COAT CARE
REGISTERED KC, FCI, AKCs
COLORS Gold

Also known in Europe as the Hungarian Wirehaired Pointer or Drotzörü Magyar Vizsla, this breed is less familiar than its shorthaired parent. However, its popularity is spreading in the United Kingdom, North America, and Australia.

BREED ORIGINS

The Hungarian Wirehaired Vizsla was developed in the early 20th century. Wanting a dog with a thicker coat and heavier frame, suitable for working in less favorable weather, breeders crossed the Vizsla with the German Wirehaired Pointer. Although it is not reliably recorded, it may be that griffon breeds, the Pudelpointer, and even the Red Setter were also used in the early stages. In all respects but the coat, the two Vizsla breeds are alike, sharing not only their looks but their deeply affectionate, gentle character and lively enthusiasm for games; they have always been part of the family.

GAINING GROUND The Wirehaired lacks an undercoat, so it is not a breed that can live outdoors. A medium-paced pointer that also retrieves well, this versatile breed is likely to spread as a hunting dog as much as a companion.

Irish Setter

ORIGIN Ireland
HEIGHT 25–27 in (64–69 cm)
WEIGHT 60–70 lb (27.2–31.8 kg)
EXERCISE LEVEL
COAT CARE
REGISTERED KC, FCI, AKCs
COLORS Red-tan

In Irish, it is Modder rhu or Madra rua, the red dog, and although it is the most recent of the nine dog breeds native to the country, it is perhaps the best known.

BREED ORIGINS

This breed is sometimes called the Irish Red Setter, in deference to its Red-and-White antecedent. The solid coat existed by the 18th century, but only became fashionable in the 19th century. In the United States there are large Irish Setters, found in show halls, and smaller Red Setters, bred to be true to the working origins. Harder to train than other gundogs, it makes a good-natured, spirited companion.

GOOD LOOKS A silky, flowing coat has made this redhead a perenially popular companion.

Labrador Retriever

ORIGIN United Kingdom
HEIGHT 22–24 in (51–61 cm)
WEIGHT 55–75 lb (24.9–34.0 kg)
EXERCISE LEVEL 🐕
COAT CARE ✎
REGISTERED KC, FCI, AKCs
COLORS Golden, chocolate, black

Anyone in search of a genial companion or family dog is likely to be advised "if in doubt, get a Lab," and it seems most do. This is undoubtedly the most popular breed in the English-speaking world.

BLACK   GOLD   DARK BROWN

BREED ORIGINS

The ancestor of this breed was the St. John's Dog, a precursor of the Newfoundland. Brought to the United Kingdom by fishermen, it was the start of the Curly-coated, Flat-coated, and Labrador Retrievers, its proven ability in pulling nets ashore by their floats now applied to safely retrieving game. Labradors were named by the early 19th century and became common by the end of the century, appearing in the United States early in the 20th century.

BREED QUALITIES

The trainable, obedient nature of this breed has made it the world's favorite assistance dog, and individuals have learned to do everything from negotiating traffic to putting their owner's cash cards into machines for them. They make wonderfully happy, exuberant family dogs, but have boundless energy and a boundless appetite.

COLOR TRENDS Brown and yellow pups occurred from the start and were eventually recognized. The yellows have become ever paler, until almost all are pale cream today, although shades down to "red fox" are allowed.

ORIGINAL COLOR Labs were at first strongly preferred in black, as shown by the first painting of one, *Cora, a Labrador Bitch* by Edwin Landseer.

IT'S NOT WORK As in many other gundog breeds, there are distinct show lines and separate, usually more rangy, working dogs. Labs from working lines have even higher energy levels. Even a show Lab will retrieve anything with gusto.

Large Munsterlander

ORIGIN Germany
HEIGHT 23–26 in (58–65 cm)
WEIGHT 64–68 lb (29.0–31.0 kg)
EXERCISE LEVEL
COAT CARE
REGISTERED KC, FCI, AKCs
COLORS Black and white

At home this is the Grosser Münsterländer, but it loses its accent abroad, and this spaniel-type German pointer has been quite a successful export. Although it is seen in modest numbers in show halls, it is appreciated as a versatile breed by hunters.

BREED ORIGINS

Ultimately these dogs are descended from medieval white or bicolored bird dogs, but the modern breed dates back to the 19th century breeding that produced the German Shorthaired, Wirehaired, and Longhaired Pointers. The last type of these is very rarely seen, but is the parent of this dog. Unwanted black-and-white puppies turned up in Longhaired Pointer litters, and in the 1920s they became a separate breed in Münster, named to distinguish them from the Small Munsterlander.

BREED QUALITIES

Field trials show this breed to be slow-maturing but worth the wait, since it works close to the hunter and is very responsive to training. It has always lived in the home, and is a calm, gentle character, reliable with children and other dogs.

BREED LOOKS The long, dense coat of this breed allows it to move through dense cover without problems, and also provides good insulation. The head should be solid black, but the rest of the coat is flecked and patched.

Small Munsterlander

ORIGIN Germany
HEIGHT 20–22 in (50–56 cm)
WEIGHT 31–35 lb (14.0–16.0 kg)
EXERCISE LEVEL
COAT CARE
REGISTERED KC, FCI, AKCs
COLORS Brown and white

Although both come from the province of Münster, where this is called the Kleiner Münsterländer, this breed is not directly related to the Large Munsterlander. The two spring from different origins and differ in color and size—although in North America this "small" breed is becoming quite large.

BREED ORIGINS

The exact origins of the Small Munsterlander are unclear. Relaxed hunting laws and many new hunters in the 19th century brought an explosion in German breeding of pointers and retrievers. Adaptable hunting dogs called Wachtelhunds or German Spaniels were recorded in Münster; the breeders involved in turning these dogs into a breed included heath poet Hermann Löns, the Baron of Bevervörde-Lohburg, and a teacher named Heitmann. Still primarily a hunting companion, these make lively, affectionate pets for active households.

OLD-FASHIONED LOOKS Bred since the 1920s to a standard written by Friedrich Jungklaus, this dog has traits that were once common in all European hunting dogs.

IN DEMAND This breed is rare beyond Germany. Only a handful of dogs have been registered so far in the United Kingdom, while in the United States, hunters snap up available dogs quickly.

Weimaraner

ORIGIN Germany
HEIGHT 23–28 in (58–71 cm)
WEIGHT 70–85 lb (31.8–38.6 kg)
EXERCISE LEVEL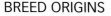
COAT CARE
REGISTERED KC, FCI, AKCs
COLORS Gray

The word "Vorstehhund," meaning pointer, is now usually dropped from this breed's name, and it is much more of an all-purpose dog, also competent in tracking and retrieving. They are sometimes nicknamed Gray Ghosts.

BREED ORIGINS
Some claim the Weimaraner is an ancient breed, discernable in a 17th-century painting by Van Dyck, but at this time it was still more a leash-hound, used to track and bring down large game. Its history only becomes certain at the start of the 19th century, when it was popular in the Weimar court of Karl August, Grand Duke of Saxe-Weimar-Eisenach, an enthusiastic huntsman. By this time, hunting of boar and stags was in decline, and a pointer for use against small game was much more useful. The older hound was crossed with Hühnerhund or bird-dog types to create the oldest of the German pointing breeds.

BREED QUALITIES
The Weimaraner is popular as a companion in many countries; overbreeding has led to temperament problems such as aggression and separation anxiety in some lines. The best Weimaraners are active, intelligent, cheerful companions, but they can be reserved with strangers.

BREED LOOKS Besides the more common shorthair, there is a longhair with a smooth or slightly wavy coat.

SPLIT PERSONALITY The Gray Ghost nickname comes not only from the breed's color but its silent, stealthy action when working. In contrast, the off-duty Weimaraner is full of bounce and enthusiasm.

Belgian Shepherd Dog

ORIGIN Belgium

HEIGHT 22–26 in (56–66 cm)

WEIGHT 44–66 lb (20.0–30.0 kg)

EXERCISE LEVEL

COAT CARE

REGISTERED KC, FCI, AKCs

COLORS Fawn with mask or traces of black overlay, black

Europe has four varieties of Chien de Berger Belge or Belgian Shepherd Dog: Groenendael, Malinois, Tervueren, and Lakenois. In North America, the first of these is called the Belgian Sheepdog.

BLACK   CREAM   RED/TAN   BLACK AND TAN

BREED ORIGINS

Across the world, herding dogs tend to have developed from local varieties without formal breeding, partly because they were the working dogs of the people, not high-status hunting dogs. At the end of the 19th century, breeders in Belgium set out to produce a small range of ideal types that could be recognized nationally: Initial lists included as many as eight different types. In 1891 Professor Adolphe Reul of the Cureghem Veterinary Medical School organized a gathering of 117 representatives of the many diverse herding dogs from across the nation. The best were chosen, and the newly formed Belgian Shepherd Dog Club began some very close interbreeding involving a few stud dogs, working to a breed standard with three coat varieties, a fourth being recognized in 1897. However, the Lakenois remains unrecognized in the United States. The question of coat colors and types has remained a cause of lively debate, but the type has always been fairly settled.

MALINOIS This variety has short hair over most of its body, very short on the head and lower legs. There is more fullness around the neck and on the back of the thighs and the tail. It is fawn overlaid with black.

LAKENOIS This variety has a rough, dry, tousled coat, never long enough for the tail to look like a plume. It is fawn, overlaid on the muzzle and the tail with traces of black.

BREED QUALITIES

All of the Belgian Shepherd types are trainable, reliable characters, making good guard dogs as long as they are not left alone too much. They are often used in police work, with the Tervueren also employed as a sniffer dog. Surprisingly well suited to apartment living, they are relatively inactive indoors, but this does not mean outdoor pursuits can be skimped; the Tervueren is perhaps the most active, but all working dogs thrive on interesting exercise.

Of the four, the Groenendael is the most popular, followed by the Tervueren. These two have a reputation for being slightly snappy, perhaps due to breeding for use in security work, and are less suitable as family pets than the others. The lighter, short-haired Malinois is less often seen, and the curly-coated Lakenois is quite rare. All are fairly healthy, although skin allergies, eye problems, and dysplasia are seen.

TERVUEREN Sporting a rich fawn coat overlaid with black, this type and the Malinois have a dark mask. Six areas must be black: The two ears, the two upper eyelids, and the two lips.

GROENENDAEL This type is a uniform shade of black. It has a long, smooth coat over the body, forming a ruff at the throat and a "jabot" or apron over the chest.

Bearded Collie

ORIGIN United Kingdom

HEIGHT 20–22 in (50–56 cm)

WEIGHT 40–66 lb (18.0–30.0 kg)

EXERCISE LEVEL

COAT CARE

REGISTERED KC, FCI, AKCs

COLORS Gray, black, fawn, brown, either solid or with white

A long coat and gentle expression give the impression that this breed is a big softie, and it does have a gentle, reliable personality. But beneath the coat is a lean body packed with spirit and energy.

BLACK　　CREAM　　GRAY　　DARK BROWN　　BLACK AND WHITE

BREED ORIGINS

According to the breed legends, a Polish sea captain traded three of his Polish Sheepdogs to a Scottish shepherd for a valuable ram and ewe in the early 16th century. When these dogs interbred with the local herding stock, the Bearded Collie breed was born. There may have been two sizes of the breed originally: A smaller, lighter one for gathering and herding in the highlands, and a heavier type for droving in the lowlands. They were used for centuries, variously called Highland Sheepdog, Highland Collie, and Hairy Moved Collie. The breed was described in the late 19th-century book *Dogs of Scotland* as "a big, rough, 'tousy' looking tyke, with a coat not unlike a doormat." They may have been involved in the creation of the Old English Sheepdog.

Although shown at the turn of the 20th century, the breed then all but vanished. After World War II a Mrs. Willison started its revival, and by the 1960s it was once again recognized and even exported to the United States, although it is still not common.

BREED QUALITIES

That long, high-maintenance coat is no fashion accessory; the weatherproof outer layer covers an insulating undercoat. The owner of a Beardie must be willing to go out in all weathers, because nothing will dissuade this dog. It is renowned for its "bounce" and apparently boundless energy, and it needs access to an outdoor space.

The breed is also famed for its cheerful, enthusiastic, humorous personality, and a tail said to never stop wagging. It thrives on human company, pines without it, and makes an excellent family dog; despite its loud bark, it is not a good watchdog. Intelligent and sometimes headstrong, it benefits enormously from training, and enjoys tracking, competitive obedience or agility trials, or simply performing tricks. Although prone to hip dysplasia, this is a generally healthy breed that lives to about 12 years.

WELL HIDDEN Although set high, the ears are pendent and lie very close to the head, giving such a smooth line that they cannot be discerned at all on a well-groomed dog.

Border Collie

ORIGIN United Kingdom
HEIGHT 18–21 in (46–54 cm)
WEIGHT 31–49 lb (14.0–22.0 kg)
EXERCISE LEVEL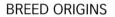
COAT CARE
REGISTERED KC, FCI, AKCs
COLORS Any solid or mixed colors, white never predominating

This intensely intelligent and boundlessly energetic breed can be hugely rewarding to own. With an active, attentive owner, it is a superb dog; with an inactive or absent owner, it is a problem.

BLACK   CREAM   GRAY   BLUE

BREED ORIGINS

Developed in the borders of England and Scotland as a working sheepdog, today this remains the most popular herding breed. Although the breed was known since the 18th century, it was only recognized by its present name in 1915.

Centuries of breeding for ability rather than looks have created a supremely intelligent, fast, and responsive dog of great stamina. This is the ultimate breed for anyone who wants to compete in agility trials, or for an active family with older children who enjoy daily games with a canine companion. It is a perfectionist and will do almost anything for praise, so is highly trainable. The only difficulty is likely to be feeding its voracious appetite for activity, so couch-potatoes need not apply. If left alone for long stretches of the working day,

Border Collies will become bored, miserable, and destructive, and the negligent owner may find that they are snappily herded around their own home.

COLLIE LOOKS Although any color is allowed, and there is a smooth-haired variety, the Border Collie is most often seen as a classic black-and-white dog with a long, insulating coat—although this is shorter in puppies.

Dog trials

Border Collies can perform outstandingly in this alternative to the "beauty contest" dog show. There are classes devoted to tunnels, gates, jumps, and slaloms, as well as obedience classes, and herding trials for working lines. To a Collie, this is not a chore, but what it lives for. Anyone considering a Border Collie should visit a dog trial and ask themselves honestly if they could keep up.

German Shepherd Dog

ORIGIN Germany

HEIGHT 22–26 in (55–65 cm)

WEIGHT 49–88 lb (22.0–40.0 kg)

EXERCISE LEVEL

COAT CARE

REGISTERED KC, FCI, AKCs

COLORS Black, gray, black with reddish-brown, brown; yellow to light gray markings

The Deutscher Schäferhund, also once called Alsatian, has served in wars, achieved Hollywood fame, and spawned two offshoot breeds, the Shiloh Shepherd and the White Swiss Shepherd Dog.

BLACK

GRAY

DARK BROWN

BLACK AND TAN

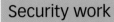

CHANGING LOOKS Breed standards have shifted over the decades, emphasizing smaller dogs with shorter, darker coats.

Security work

The German Shepherd was used as a military dog in World War I, and taken home by soldiers returning to the United Kingdom and the United States. Since then it has proved itself unparalleled in intelligence and trainability, and "police dog" became a synonym for the breed.

EVER READY The large pricked ears and clean-cut, tapering head mean that even at rest these dogs look alert and primed to spring into action.

BREED ORIGINS

The "wolf-like dog of the country around the Rhine" was noted by Roman historian Tacitus nearly 2,000 years ago, but the German Shepherd is usually dated to the 1890s and credited largely to Max von Stephanitz. He owned Horand von Grafrath, the founding male, reputed to have a recent wolf cross in his parentage. Thuringian dogs gave the upright ears and wolf-like appearance, while Württemburger dogs were used for their temperament and speed.

BREED QUALITIES

Today, North American dogs have a very sloping stance, quite distinct from the more level European lines. Dogs from the old East Germany are said to resemble the original most closely, and working dogs are largely drawn from east European lines. Hip and digestive disorders remain a problem despite the best efforts of good breeders, and while some individuals make excellent family dogs, caution is advisable.

Old English Sheepdog

ORIGIN United Kingdom
HEIGHT 22–24 in (56–60 cm)
WEIGHT 65–66 lb (29.5–30.0 kg)
EXERCISE LEVEL
COAT CARE
REGISTERED KC, FCI, AKCs
COLORS Gray, blue, with limited white markings

Famous in much of the world as the "Dulux dog," this profusely shaggy breed has a personality to match its cuddly looks. This is a loyal and adaptable companion.

GRAY   BLUE

BREED ORIGINS
First bred selectively in the 19th century, mostly in southwestern England, the Old English may be descended from continental breeds such as the Briard, or even the Polish Lowland Sheepdog. Usually docked, it was also called the Bobtail. It was originally an aggressive and snappish character, but careful breeding has rendered it a biddable family dog, although it still makes a good guard.

SHAGGY DOG Square and thick-set, this is a sturdy breed with a rolling gait. A monthly clipping helps to keep it tidy.

Puli

ORIGIN Hungary
HEIGHT 14–18 in (36–45 cm)
WEIGHT 22–33 lb (10.0–15.0 kg)
EXERCISE LEVEL
COAT CARE
REGISTERED KC, FCI, AKCs
COLORS Black, black with rust or gray shadings, fawn with black mask, white

This lively and intelligent little dog, originally a herder, is the best-known of the Hungarian breeds. Aided by its eye-catching coat, it has successfully made the shift to family companion.

BLACK   CREAM   GOLD

BREED ORIGINS
This breed's ancestors were probably large stock-guarding dogs that came to Hungary with the Magyars around 1,000 years ago. Black dogs were preferred, probably because they are easy to spot among sheep. The smaller Puli emerged as an agile herder, while the larger Komondor was used for guarding. Today the Puli makes an adaptable companion and guard dog, and does well in obedience trials.

CORDED COAT
Once it is worked into pencil-thick cords, the coat needs no daily grooming but it does require regular bathing and drying. The Puli is remarkably adaptable to a wide range of climates, and enjoys swimming—it is also known as the Hungarian Water Dog.

Rough Collie

ORIGIN United Kingdom
HEIGHT 20–24 in (50–60 cm)
WEIGHT 40–66 lb (18.0–30.0 kg)
EXERCISE LEVEL
COAT CARE
REGISTERED KC, FCI, AKCs
COLORS Sable, sable and white, blue merle, tricolor

One of the world's most popular breeds, this looks too elegant for herding work, although it retains its original abilities. First made fashionable at home by Queen Victoria, in the 20th century it became familiar to a wider audience as "Lassie."

BLUE

BLACK, WHITE AND TAN

BREED ORIGINS

For centuries, this was an obscure Scottish herding dog, producing both long- and occasional shorthaired dogs. It was somewhat smaller than it is today, with a less luxuriant coat and shorter nose. Then it was crossed with Borzois, giving a taller, leaner build and an aristocratic face, and has been at home in the show ring ever since.

BREED QUALITIES

Intelligent enough to work as a rescue and guide dog, this amiable breed makes a good family dog, but occasional snappish individuals do occur. Its popularity makes it essential to buy a pup screened for eye defects and hip problems from a reputable breeder.

COLLIE COAT This is an active breed that needs plenty of free running, but the spectacular coat is the greatest commitment. Daily grooming is needed, with more thorough attention weekly. In Europe the Rough and Smooth Collies are recognized as separate breeds; in North America one breed with two coat lengths is recognized.

Welsh Corgis

ORIGIN United Kingdom
HEIGHT 10–13 in (25–32 cm)
WEIGHT 20–26 lb (9.0–12.0 kg)
EXERCISE LEVEL
COAT CARE
REGISTERED KC, FCI
COLORS Red, sable, fawn, black and tan, white allowed (Pembroke); all colors (Cardigan)

Although the Pembroke and the Cardigan Corgi remain distinct breeds with their own standards, they are very similar, a result of crossbreeding between them until the 20th century.

BLACK   RED/TAN   BLACK AND WHITE   BLACK, WHITE, AND TAN   BLACK BRINDLE

BREED ORIGINS

Romantics claim that Corgis arrived with the Celts over 2,000 years ago. Others believe they are descended from Swedish Vallhund stock arriving with the Vikings a little over 1,000 years ago, although it may be that the Vallhund is descended from Welsh dogs. The name corgi is recorded in *A Dictionary in Englyshe and Welshe* published in 1574, as "Korgi ne gostoc, Corgi or curre dogge," meaning working or guarding dog.

This was primarily a cattle-droving breed or "heeler," left unemployed by transportation developments in the 20th century. Only when the future

Queen Elizabeth acquired her first Corgis did the breed come back to popularity, this time as a companion breed.

BREED QUALITIES

Heelers had to be bold enough to run behind the feet of the cattle and nip their heels, low and robust enough to roll away from the resulting kicks, and determined enough to go back for more. These qualities make them lively companions, but too stubborn and snappish to be good family dogs.

CARDIGAN CORGI The ears of the Cardigan type are large and the nose less pointed than that of the Pembroke, although never blunt. The coat is hard and short or medium in length.

PEMBROKE CORGI Sturdily built but smaller than the Cardigan type, the Pembroke has a foxy, pointed face and a medium length coat. Pembroke Corgis often have naturally short tails; those with long tails were traditionally docked.

Akita

ORIGIN Japan
HEIGHT 24–28 in (60–70 cm)
WEIGHT 75–110 lb (34.0–50.0 kg)
EXERCISE LEVEL
COAT CARE
REGISTERED KC, FCI, AKCs
COLORS White, white and red, fawn, or brindle; any color (United States)

The largest of the Japanese breeds, this originates in Akita prefecture on the island of Honshu. It has developed along quite different lines in Japan and Europe and in the United States.

GOLD AND WHITE   TAN AND WHITE   BLACK BRINDLE

BREED ORIGINS

Used for hunting and fighting in the 19th century, after World War II, the Akita was low in numbers and included German Shepherd crosses. In Japan, breeders worked to restore the old breed, but hybrid dogs were taken home by American soldiers. The breed is now a Natural Monument in its homeland. All Akitas are staunch, fearless fighters that need experienced owners.

DIFFERENCES
The American Akita is larger than the lines from Japan and Europe, and is allowed in a wider range of colors. The two types are not mutually recognized.

Alaskan Malamute

ORIGIN United States
HEIGHT 23–26 in (58–65 cm)
WEIGHT 75–86 lb (34.0–39.0 kg)
EXERCISE LEVEL
COAT CARE
REGISTERED KC, FCI, AKCs
COLORS White with shades of gray or red

This was the preferred sled dog of North America for thousands of years. Its name comes from the Mahlemuts, the Alaskan tribe that kept it. Packs have been used in many polar expeditions.

BLACK AND WHITE   TAN AND WHITE

BREED ORIGINS

Recent genetic research confirmed that this is one of the world's oldest dog breeds. It is an intelligent and tireless pack dog. Loyal, affectionate, and gentle, Malamutes need plenty of work if they are not to become bored and destructive.

PRACTICAL STANDARDS Malamutes' sizes can vary widely, but the breed standards are healthy sizes ideal for pulling work in a matched team.

American Eskimo (Standard)

ORIGIN United States
HEIGHT Over 15 in (38 cm)
WEIGHT 20–35 lb (9.1–16.0 kg)
EXERCISE LEVEL
COAT CARE
REGISTERED AKCs
COLORS White

Not to be confused with the larger white Canadian Eskimo Dog recognized in the United Kingdom, this spirited spitz comes in Standard, Miniature, and Toy sizes, packing all the punch of a typical sled-puller in a compact parcel.

BREED ORIGINS

Despite its name, this breed is not actually descended from Eskimo or Inuit dogs, but white spitz dogs brought by European settlers and descended from the German Spitz; anti-German feelings during World War I led to a swift change of identity. Despite its diminutive appearance, this dog has earned its keep: It won popularity performing in the Barnum and Bailey Circus, and does well in obedience and agility classes. It makes a noisy watchdog, but may not be appreciated by close neighbours. Some individuals are shy or overly aggressive, but in general this is a good family dog.

SNOW DOG This is a healthy and long-lived little dog that lasts into its teens. The thick double coat is fairly easy to groom, but there is a tendency to brown tear staining on the face.

Australian Kelpie

ORIGIN Australia
HEIGHT 17–20 in (43–51 cm)
WEIGHT 24–44 lb (11.0–20.0 kg)
EXERCISE LEVEL
COAT CARE
REGISTERED FCI, AKCs
COLORS Black, blue, red, fawn, chocolate, black and tan, red, red and tan

Australia's most popular working dog, this breed is known and shown around the world. In the United Kingdom it is only eligible for trials, but it excels in these, showing its collie heritage.

BLACK   BLUE   RED/TAN   DARK BROWN   BLACK AND TAN

BREED ORIGINS

There have always been tales that the Kelpie contains dingo blood, and dingo crosses might have been made but not admitted; however, the breed's remarkable trainability makes this claim dubious. Collies from northern England provided much of its stock, with a black-and-tan bitch named Kelpie giving fresh genes and the breed name. Kelpies are tenacious, intelligent, and enthusiastic workers, described as workaholics. They might be regarded as Australia's Border Collie, and need a similar level of commitment to an active and interesting life if they are not to be bored, snappy, and destructive.

BEAUTY OR BRAINS? Today the Kelpie is split into working and show lines. Those who breed working Kelpies for their abilities have less regard for looks.

Bernese Mountain Dog

ORIGIN Switzerland
HEIGHT 23–28 in (58–70 cm)
WEIGHT 88–100 lb (40.0–45.0 kg)
EXERCISE LEVEL
COAT CARE
REGISTERED KC, FCI, AKCs
COLORS Tricolor

The Berner Sennenhund is the largest of the four tricolored Swiss mountain or cattle dogs, and the only one with a long coat. Historically used for herding and pulling carts, it is now a well-established companion breed.

BREED ORIGINS

The origins of these breeds are ancient, and Roman mastiffs are among the likely ancestors. The number of foreign dogs brought into Switzerland in the 19th century threatened the native breeds' survival: Together with the Appenzell, Entelbuch, and Great Swiss, this breed was saved by the efforts of breeders led by Professor Albert Heim. It is a powerful but affectionate and reliable breed. Tragically, many die young through cancer; the average lifespan has fallen in recent years and is now somewhere around seven years.

BIG AND BOLD Despite its size and sturdy build, the Bernese has historically been a surprisingly agile breed.

Boxer

ORIGIN Germany
HEIGHT 21–25 in (53–63 cm)
WEIGHT 53–70 lb (24.0–32.0 kg)
EXERCISE LEVEL
COAT CARE
REGISTERED KC, FCI, AKCs
COLORS Shades of fawn, brindle; solid or with white

More accurately known as the Deutscher Boxer, this breed is often seen with cropped ears in the United States. The natural look shows its playful, intelligent—if stubborn—nature far better.

RED/TAN	GOLD	BLACK BRINDLE

BREED ORIGINS

The Brabant Bullenbeisser and similar hunting breeds are the immediate ancestors of the Boxer; their task was to seize large game and hold onto it until the huntsmen arrived; hence the broad, shortened muzzle. Bred by huntsmen, for their working qualities, they were variable in type. In the late 19th century, breeders created this physically consistent type for showing. Highly trainable and popular for military and police work, they are nonetheless clowns at heart, and make good family dogs.

TALL TAILS The Boxer was traditionally docked, but this has now changed in Europe. It was feared that the tail would prove variable, but the standard for a high but not curled over tail has now been set.

British Bulldog

ORIGIN United Kingdom
HEIGHT 12–14 in (30–36 cm)
WEIGHT 51–55 lb (23.0–25.0 kg)
EXERCISE LEVEL
COAT CARE
REGISTERED KC, FCI, AKCs
COLORS Solid fawn, red, brindle, or with a black mask or white

Recognized by registries simply as the Bulldog, this iconic breed is as British as the John Bull character that it so often accompanied in patriotic cartoons.

TAN AND WHITE   BLACK BRINDLE

BREED ORIGINS
The name "bulldog" has been in use since the 17th century, but the term originally described crosses of bear-baiting mastiffs and tenacious terriers. Bred to hang on to a bull for all they were worth in a fight, they had the short, broad jaw also seen in German Bullenbeissers that performed the same role in the hunt. But these early dogs were lighter, more athletic examples than the breed we have today, with a true fighting dog temperament.

When bull baiting was banned in the 19th century, those who rescued the breed from oblivion created a new type of dog, not only much heavier set but utterly reformed in character.

BREED QUALITIES
Today's Bulldog is almost without exception tolerant and gentle. It might be said that it simply had no energy left for aggression: Breathing disorders and heart trouble plagued the breed. Of late, responsible breeders have begun to reject the extreme looks that exacerbated these conditions, and Bulldogs can now look forward to healthier and longer lives. Their characters are more lively, but still as sweet.

GOING TO EXTREMES The large heads of Bulldogs mean the breed has a high incidence of caesarian births, while the deep folds on the face need scrupulous care to keep skin problems at bay. But for their fans, there is nothing to beat the Bulldog breed.

Cane Corso Italiano

ORIGIN Italy
HEIGHT 24–27 in (60–68 cm)
WEIGHT 88–110 lb (40.0–50.0 kg)
EXERCISE LEVEL
COAT CARE
REGISTERED FCI, AKCs
COLORS Black, shades of gray or fawn, brindle

Also used for herding and hunting, this breed is primarily a guard. Its name translates approximately as Italian guard dog; it is also called the Cane di Macellaio, Sicilian Branchiero, and Italian Mastiff.

BLACK   GRAY   GOLD   BLACK BRINDLE

BREED ORIGINS

The ultimate ancestor of the Corso is the Roman mastiff. The lighter examples of this type were used not only as military attack dogs but in large game hunting. A natural continuation, the Corso has been kept throughout Italian history and across the country, although in most recent times the highest numbers have been found in southern Italy. A quiet, intelligent breed that is loyal and protective of its home and family, the Corso needs sound training to insure that it is not overly suspicious around strangers.

ROBUST BUILD Traditionally docked and often seen with cropped ears, the breed now sports a more natural look in Europe. It does suffer the same health concerns as other large breeds, particularly with regard to joints.

Chow Chow

ORIGIN China
HEIGHT 18–22 in (45–56 cm)
WEIGHT 44–70 lb (20.0–32.0 kg)
EXERCISE LEVEL
COAT CARE
REGISTERED KC, FCI, AKCs
COLORS White, cream, fawn, red, blue, black

Whether smooth or rough coated, the Chow Chow looks like no other breed. It is one of the most ancient of all breeds, and has a varied history covering every role from working dog to dinner.

BLACK   CREAM   RED/TAN

BREED ORIGINS

Genetic research confirms the Chow as an ancient type. In Asia it was used for hunting, sled pulling, herding, and guarding, while its fur was valued and its flesh was eaten. It came to the West from China in the 19th century.

This breed is still more than capable of fulfilling its historic guarding role, although it has not found favor as a herding or hunting dog in the West. Although breeders have been working to produce a

Chow with more of a laid-back, family dog nature, it remains for the most part an independent, stubborn, and slightly suspicious breed. Early socialization and a strong owner are vital.

CONSTANT CARE The Chow is prone to a range of joint problems. The coat is also a serious commitment, since it sheds heavily.

Dalmatian

ORIGIN Croatia or India
HEIGHT 21–24 in (54–61 cm)
WEIGHT 55–66 lb (25.0–30.0 kg)
EXERCISE LEVEL
COAT CARE
REGISTERED KC, FCI, AKCs
COLORS White with black or liver spots

Instantly recognizable, famous for one hundred and one reasons, the Dalmatian or Dalmatinac has in its time been a hunting dog, a herder, a ratter, and a carriage dog.

BREED ORIGINS

Dogs like this have been known in Dalmatia, now Croatia, for 4,000 years. But the Bengal Pointer, a similar dog from India, was known in the United Kingdom in 1700: Which is the ancestor of the breed we know today is not certain. Deafness and urinary stones are health issues, and males especially can be aggressive—early training is vital, as well as a long daily run.

LOOK DEEPER The smart coat and fame of the breed attract many owners, but some are just not prepared for the time and energy demanded, particularly by a young dog.

Poodle (Standard)

ORIGIN Germany
HEIGHT 15–24 in (38–60 cm)
WEIGHT 45–70 lb (20.5–32.0 kg)
EXERCISE LEVEL
COAT CARE
REGISTERED KC, FCI, AKCs
COLORS Any solid color

This breed's origins are acknowledged in its name, from the old German word *pudeln*, "to splash"; it is called the Caniche, or duck dog, in France. This practical retriever can be a smart companion.

BLACK　　　CREAM　　　BLUE　　　GOLD　　　DARK BROWN

BREED ORIGINS
This breed can be traced back at least to the Middle Ages, and probably arose in Germany, eastern Europe, or even Asia. It is officially recognized as French, however, and in France it developed into the modern sizes of Standard and the smaller Miniature and Toy types. It worked in French circuses, its intelligence and trainability making it hugely popular, and as a truffle hound. This is a healthy, able, adaptable breed, and certainly no fluffy toy.

CONTINENTAL AND LION CLIPS Although these look ornamental, their original purpose was to reduce the resistance of the coat in the water but leave the chest and the leg joints insulated.

SHORT CLIPS All-over clips are now allowed for showing. This simpler look is far easier for most owners to maintain, and allows the breed a little more of its natural dignity in everyday life.

STANDARDS FOR STANDARDS The allowed sizes for the different Poodle classes vary among registries, with FCI starting at a threshhold 3 in (8 cm) taller than others.

Pyrenean Mastiff

ORIGIN Spain

HEIGHT 28–32 in (72–80 cm)

WEIGHT 121–165 lb (55.0–75.0 kg)

EXERCISE LEVEL

COAT CARE

REGISTERED FCI

COLORS White with gray, golden yellow, brown, black, silver, beige, sand, or marbled

A herd and farm guarding breed, the Mastin del Pireneo, sometimes called the Mastin d'Aragon, could take on bears and wolves. This robust, trainable breed makes a good guard for rural households.

GOLD AND WHITE

BLACK AND WHITE

TAN AND WHITE

BREED ORIGINS

Phoenician traders probably brought the first mastiffs to Spain from Asia thousands of years ago. This dog developed in the southeastern Pyrenees, and guarded both flocks and the home. A large breed with a deep voice, a strong protective instinct, and inherent reluctance to back down, it is not ideal for urban life. Sometimes aggressive toward other dogs, it controls its power.

UNDEREXPOSED BREED This is a solid, imposing dog but never gives the impression of being overly heavy or slow. It is one of the rarer mastiff breeds, perhaps overshadowed by—or confused with—the Pyrenean Mountain Dog.

Pyrenean Mountain Dog

ORIGIN France

HEIGHT 26–32 in (65–80 cm)

WEIGHT 121–165 lb (55.0–75.0 kg)

EXERCISE LEVEL

COAT CARE

REGISTERED KC, FCI, AKCs

COLORS White, white with very limited gray, pale yellow, or orange patches

Originating on the French side of the Pyrenees, this dauntless, intelligent breed is called the Chien de Montagne des Pyrénées in France and is also known as the Great Pyrenees in some registries.

GOLD AND WHITE

BIG AND BOLD The sheer size and weight of this breed make it unsuitable for city living. Like other large breeds, it is susceptible to joint problems, and it can develop skin problems in the heat.

BREED ORIGINS

Probably descended from ancient Asian mastiffs, this dog is recorded as a herd and home guarding breed by the Middle Ages, and was found at the French royal court in the 17th century. Nearly extinct in the early 20th century, it is now established across Europe and North America. Early examples were markedly wary, but breeding for companionship has mellowed the character.

Rhodesian Ridgeback

ORIGIN South Africa
HEIGHT 24–27 in (60–69 cm)
WEIGHT 70–80 lb (32.0–36.0 kg)
EXERCISE LEVEL
COAT CARE
REGISTERED KC, FCI, AKCs
COLORS Light wheaten to red wheaten

The only registered breed indigenous to southern Africa, the Rhodesian is characterized by the stripe of hair that grows forward along its spine that also gives the breed its name. It was believed unique in this trait until the discovery of the Thai Ridgeback.

BREED ORIGINS

Dogs with this characteristic ridge of hair, kept for hunting by the Hottentots, interbred with settlers' hounds and mastiffs in the 19th century. The resulting breed was used in pairs or trios to find lions for hunters, and an old name for the Ridgeback is the African Lion Hound. With changing attitudes to wildlife, the breed has moved into the home, and it makes a loyal guard dog or companion. It is a dignified breed that can be aloof with strangers, and it prefers to have its owners to itself, rather than sharing them with disruptive children or other dogs.

KEPT IN TRIM The first standard for the Ridgeback, written in the 1920s, was based on that of the Dalmatian. It placed the emphasis on agility and elegance, producing a breed of great endurance and speed.

Rottweiler

ORIGIN Germany
HEIGHT 23–27 in (58–69 cm)
WEIGHT 90–110 lb (41.0–50.0 kg)
EXERCISE LEVEL
COAT CARE
REGISTERED KC, FCI, AKCs
COLORS Black and tan

Originally a cattle dog and hauler of carts, later a guard, military dog, and police dog, the Rottweiler was never, as is sometimes asserted, a fighting dog. This belief is just part of the sometimes unfavorable, often unfair, reputation this breed has gathered.

Dangerous dogs?

Rottweilers are intelligent and highly trainable, and a well-socialized Rottie in the hands of an experienced and sensible owner is a fine dog. However, there is no denying that they are protective, assertive, and can show a temper.

BREED ORIGINS

The Rottweiler's earliest ancestors were probably Roman mastiffs; an ancient military route ran through the town of Rottweil in southern Germany. They were popular on farms, and were also known as "Rottweil butchers' dogs" because of their usefulness in controlling animals at slaughter, pulling carts, and guard duties. Numbers declined greatly in the 19th century, but they were saved by proving their efficiency

CATCH THEM YOUNG How a breed like a Rottweiler is brought up has a great effect on its behavior. Puppies that are constantly exposed to human play, children, and other animals are very different from guard dogs kept outside.

when tested for their potential as police dogs. Now they are recognized as guards around the world, but seen with less favor as companions. Their size and weight alone make them a better choice as a guard than as a family dog around small children.

BIG AND BRAVE Powerful and impressive in build, the Rottweiler unfortunately suffers the dysplasia problems almost inevitable in larger breeds. The tail was customarily docked in the past, but is now left natural in Europe.

St. Bernard

ORIGIN Switzerland

HEIGHT 26–36 in (65–90 cm)

WEIGHT 100–300 lb (45.0–136.0 kg)

EXERCISE LEVEL

COAT CARE

REGISTERED KC, FCI, AKCs

COLORS White with reddish-brown patches or mantle

Regarded as the Swiss national breed, these massive dogs are also called St. Bernhardshund or Bernhardiner, and have been known as Saint Dogs—still sometimes used in North America— Alpenmastiff, and Barry Dogs.

BREED ORIGINS

These dogs are descended from Swiss farm breeds, but their original ancestors were Roman mastiffs. They probably arrived via the most ancient pass through the Western Alps, the Great St. Bernard Pass. In 1049, monks founded a hospice there named after St. Bernard of Menthon, and since at least the 17th century, mastiffs lived there as companions and guards, hauling carts and creating paths through deep snow. They became legendary rescue dogs after Napoleon's army went through the pass in 1800.

BREED QUALITIES

These lugubrious-looking dogs are gentle, friendly, loyal, and obedient. Their size makes them unsuitable for many homes, but their ponderous movements mean they are unlikely to bowl children over. Like many large breeds, they are prone to bloat and joint problems.

START SLOW Big dogs like the St. Bernard take as much as 18 months to become fully physically mature. Exercise should be carefully monitored while their bones are still growing.

LESS IS MORE There are two coats: This shorthaired or *stockhaar* has a dense double coat and was more used for work in the snow. The medium-length, straight to slightly wavy coat of the longhair could gather icicles.

Samoyed

ORIGIN Northern Russia/Siberia
HEIGHT 18–22 in (46–56 cm)
WEIGHT 50–66 lb (23.0–30.0 kg)
EXERCISE LEVEL
COAT CARE
REGISTERED KC, FCI, AKCs
COLORS White, cream, white and biscuit

Called the Samoiedskaïa Sabaka in their native land, but affectionately known as the Sammy, these smiling dogs were the working companions of the nomadic, reindeer-herding Samoyed peoples. They were once generally called Bjelkier or Voinaika.

BREED ORIGINS

Samoyedic peoples have been in Siberia for some 2,000 years. Their dogs were essential to their lifestyle, just like the Malamute in Alaska or Lapphund in Finland. They would herd reindeer, sometimes pull sleds, and sleep alongside their owners for warmth. Over the centuries, they acquired an almost mythical reputation for their abilities and loyalty. Pioneering Norwegian explorer Fridtjof Nansen took a team of 28 over the polar ice in the 1890s, and his praise of the breed influenced other explorers to use it, including Amundsen when he reached the South Pole in 1911.

BREED QUALITIES

These dogs always lived close to their owners, and as a result thrive on human company, with a friendly greeting for all. Established as good-natured family dogs in many countries, they are full of energy and need an active life to keep them occupied. They can suffer an inherited kidney problem.

COLD PROOF The double coat is water repellent on top, impenetrably wooly beneath. Black skin resists snow glare, and the tail covers the nose when sleeping, warming the inhaled air.

MAN'S BEST FRIEND With a smiling face and a nature that "displays affection to all mankind," this is a companion, not a guard.

Shar Pei

ORIGIN China
HEIGHT 18–20 in (45–50 cm)
WEIGHT 45–60 lb (20.5–27.5 kg)
EXERCISE LEVEL
COAT CARE
REGISTERED KC, FCI, AKCs
COLORS Any solid color except white

This breed is named in China for its harsh coat: Shar Pei means "sand skin." But when the breed became fashionable in the West in the 1980s, it was the wrinkles that caught the imagination.

BLACK   GRAY   BLUE   RED/TAN   GOLD

BREED ORIGINS
The Shar Pei may have existed for over 2,000 years, kept on farms for hunting and guarding. More recently it was used in fights, and it can be stubborn and aggressive. The communist regime nearly saw the demise of the dog, but exports from Hong Kong in the 1970s saved it. There are hereditary problems with skin allergies and ingrowing eyelashes: Choose breeders carefully.

FIGHTING COAT
There are two lengths of coat: The short horse coat seen here and the longer brush or bear. Loose skin and a prickly coat were good defences in dog fights, but some Shar Peis are more dramatically wrinkled than others.

Shiba Inu

ORIGIN Japan
HEIGHT 13–16 in (34–41 cm)
WEIGHT 15–24 lb (7.0–11.0 kg)
EXERCISE LEVEL
COAT CARE
REGISTERED KC, FCI, AKCs
COLORS Red, red overlaid with black, black and tan, white

This is the smallest of Japan's native breeds, and its name describes it in minimal terms: *Shiba* means "small," and *inu*—or sometimes *ken*, another reading of the same *kanji*—simply means "dog."

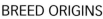

RED/TAN   BLACK AND TAN

BREED ORIGINS
Small dogs of this type have been present in Japan for millennia, and used to hunt small animals and birds. Pure specimens became scarce through crossing with imported English gundogs in the 19th century. In the 1920s, work to conserve them began, and in 1937 the breed was designated a Natural Monument. A quiet and loyal breed, they can be aloof with strangers.

ANCIENT PATTERN
In all colors, the Shiba Inu has a pattern called *urajiro* or "white beneath." The coat is light on the underparts and has light areas on the sides of the muzzle and the cheeks.

Siberian Husky

ORIGIN Siberia

HEIGHT 20–24 in (50–60 cm)

WEIGHT 35–60 lb (16.0–27.5 kg)

EXERCISE LEVEL 🐕

COAT CARE ✂️

REGISTERED KC, FCI, AKCs

COLORS Any color

One of the lighter sled-pulling breeds, the Siberian Husky has become more famous as a breed in Alaska than in its original homeland. For a time it was the ultimate racing dog.

BLACK   GRAY   GOLD AND WHITE   TAN AND WHITE

BREED ORIGINS

These dogs were used for centuries by the Chukchi people of Siberia for sled pulling and reindeer herding. DNA analysis has confirmed it as one of the oldest breeds in existence. It was brought to Alaska by fur traders for arctic races, and used by Peary in his trip to the North Pole in 1909, but won most publicity and popularity in the 1925 serum run to Nome, or Great Race of Mercy, when teams of sled dogs carried diphtheria antitoxin to the isolated

town of Nome, traveling 674 miles (1,085 km) in a record-breaking five and a half days to halt an epidemic.

BREED QUALITIES

Lighter than most other sled-pulling breeds, the Husky is characterized by a seemingly effortless gait and enormous stamina. These qualities mean it is a breed for the active, and left alone it can be destructive. They are generally cheerful dogs, gentle and friendly.

LOOK LIVELY Huskies are good-natured, but their intelligence can incline them to mischief, so owners need to be as alert as their dogs.

SIBERIAN LOOKS The breed has a tendency to blue in one or both eyes, but this is by no means universal. The thick coat is fairly tangle free, but needs plenty of combing when it molts.

INDEX